To Form a Perfect Union

To Form a Perfect Union

The Forgotten American Social Contract

Mark Smith

Copyright©2020 Mark Smith
All rights reserved.

No part of this book may be reproduced, scanned, or distributed in any printed or electronic form without permission or as allowed under copyright law.

The author can be reached at:
TheLostAmericanContract@gmail.com

Dedication

To Robert A. Smith
(June 3, 1933 – May 1, 2013)

History teacher and sportswriter who, in his wisdom, thought it more prudent to read us bedtime stories about the American Revolution than Puff the Magic Dragon.

Acknowledgments

I would like to thank Barbara Corrigan CPA, MBA; CSM David F. Smith (USA Ret.); Polly J. Smith, PhD; Rich Minucci (USAF); Jack McArdle; Kat Andonucci; Dave Putnam (USN); Ed Gregory; Craig Simonsen; LTC Dana Goulette (USA Ret.); COL Suzanne Goulette (USA Ret.); and Fred Andersen for their support, critiques, prodding, and feedback without which this work would not have been possible.

Contents

Introduction

A long, long time ago a few men had a dream of people living their lives uninhibited by kings, czars, or any such government. Through hardship, war, and debate, those men forged upon this land a society so unique it was dubbed "The Great Experiment" by Alex de Tocqueville in his study of the American republican representative democracy. So impactful was his work, it was immediately popular in Europe and America and remains a classical work that is still required reading for undergraduates focusing on political or social sciences. While the building blocks of our democracy enthralled the world, many people of the times failed to understand the American system and many more thought it would collapse after a short time. Even our founders, to some extent, didn't believe the initial structure of society would last unchanged far into the future. They believed that they merely laid a foundation upon which successive generations would build a stronger, more robust, and libertarian society.

For a while we progressed and evolved in our perfecting of this experiment, sometimes at great cost. As our lives have become less and less burdened by survival and we tap more and more into the luxury of free time, our progress seems to have waned and we have forgotten the few fundamental premises of our experiment; we have become overly and unnecessarily self-centric unleashing our personal emotions upon principles that require reason. In doing so, we have fractured the pane of our society into shards that not even the best of puzzlers can put back together.

The fallout has been great divisiveness and an over-reliance on government to provide solutions to issues that are best left with the people. In stark opposition to our origins, we prefer to surrender liberties rather than to exert ourselves in efforts to remedy these issues. Born of a bottom up society, we, either through apathy, laziness, or ignorance, thirst for a top driven structure. We want someone to tell us what to do. It is a safe—albeit temporary—illusion. We can always have someone to blame for our circumstances. Absolved of any personal responsibility, we point to "them" for our own failings.

No one wants to hear this. We see ourselves in a filtered, idyllic mirror. "I'm not like that," we say, but "they" are. Whether a person is of "us" or "them," what seems to be missing in present day America is an understanding of the underlying social contract which drives the experiment in its successes. Commentators over the last century would have you believe that events and history re-forge that contract from time to time. This is like building a house on sand. A shifting foundation makes for an unstable structure. Rather, we should erect a structure on something immutable, unchangeable, and constant throughout time.

The classical writers of social theory and social thought spent much of their time trying to dissect the psyche of the human animal. It was only after a thorough understanding of who we are as a species and what is our nature that they could begin to postulate about how societies were best maintained. No matter our world view—Christian, Islam, Buddhist, Hindi, Animalism, Atheist—we all acknowledge that everything has a specific nature which defines it as a separate and distinct part of the world. We know what it is by its nature. On occasion there are anomalies, but these outliers are so few and far between that we rarely consider re-defining an entire category. Humans are no exception. We possess a nature that we, through our sentience, realize is flawed and so strive to control and hone ourselves, through discipline, into a better, more perfect version of ourselves.

What is at the heart of human nature? Perhaps the simplest response is: *A desire for liberty; an inherent understanding of right and wrong*. These have not changed over time and best serve as the cornerstones of any social contract. How we go about achieving them may change over time and may be the cause and consequence of events that we deem landmarks in our history, but everyone born into our species will be born with these qualities. Societies differentiate themselves in how they manage these qualities and to what degree they express—or repress—them.

Our society is no different. Our founders were much more in touch with the writings and thoughts of the classical social theorists—Hobbes, Descartes, Rousseau, Kant—than we are today. Recent commentators would have us believe that our social successes and failures can be explained through the migration of time and technology. That approach seems to ignore human nature as the common denominator which drives all these things. In the end, this social theory offers a slap on the back for those few social advances we have made while providing an excuse for the more frequent failures.

We are lost. We are the forgotten Americans. At our core we want to be the person that does what's right. We want the ability to express ourselves in thought and action to the extent society allows. We want to be as free from regulations, laws, mandates, and restrictions as possibly can be had in our democratic system. But the path seems obscured and we are having trouble navigating through the fog that surrounds us. We need a compass.

Shooting an azimuth in our society is difficult at best. Each of us is a foreigner or a descendant of a foreigner. Even the Native Americans were immigrants at one point. While we have converged in many ways to become a more unified society, we still retain—oftentimes proudly—some customs and beliefs from our ancestors that will forever prevent us from being completely homogenous. In his 1908 play of the same name, Israel Zangwill described our society as a "Melting Pot." A useful image for the time. But looking out over the hundred years since, we can be described more ideally as a mixing pot of inert elements: We exist alongside other elements without changing the basic properties of either them or ourselves. In essence, this may have been an overarching point of the Great Experiment and one which seems to have been lost on recent generations. An important key to the re-unification of our society is to, somehow, get back to the concept of co-existing without one faction forcing the assimilation of another or allowing the values of any one faction to overwrite those values on all others.

In the course of two generations our nation has become more and more polarized, more and more divisive. The enemy moved from an external one to an internal one. The collective "we" heard during the Cold War has been supplanted by "them" and "us." Never has the rift between "them" and "us" been so vast than after the election of 2016. We, as a culture and as a country, are being ripped apart at the seams. And for no esoteric reason. How did we get this far down the rabbit hole? Why haven't we done something to staunch our slide into anarchy and disarray? The only logical reason for a people not to do what they can to avoid their destruction is that they don't know how. They need a "Step 1." In our case, we have forgotten why we came together in the first place and what we should expect from each other. To right the ship, we need to begin by becoming reacquainted with our social contract.

To accomplish this seemingly Herculean feat, we need to get back to basics. Dig through the dust and debris and find, again, our foundations. What we will almost certainly find etched on the American cornerstone is something akin to: *Age Recte* (Do what's right). Very simple to say; very difficult to do. While people know what is the right thing to do, they often don't do it or pretend they didn't know what to do. In that respect and more so in recent times, someone needs to compel them. Often it only takes a little push and not a whack on the head with a stick. Given a choice, people would rather be rewarded than punished. But we cannot dismiss that we, as humans, possess no small amount of herd mentality; we tend to behave like the majority around us if for no other reason than to satisfy our innate desire to be accepted. That can be for good or that can be for bad. Freeing ourselves from that slave mentality is certainly a key factor in determining what is right and doing it. Our "Step 1" is to look at our American social contract.

In the pages that follow, we will look at of what that social contract consists and how we can apply it to key controversial issues. Paraphrased, Occam's Razer says, "the simplest solution is usually the best solution." Boiling things down to their primordial elements generally provides better insights than trying to wrangle with high-minded abstractions. If we follow the common thread in the formation and evolution of our society—or any flourishing society—it comes down to three little words: Do what's right.

This is the underlying mantra of this work. It appears so frequently that one may get tired of reading it. And a lot of what is said may seem obvious. Hopefully, it is. The purpose is not so much to educate as it is to reset the reader's mindset with respect to who we are as a nation and what role the reader plays in that. In some cases, it won't be pleasant, and many will bristle at one thing or another. The goal isn't to convince individuals of any one specific way forward—there are several equally valid paths that lead to the same place—but to try to instill a sense of perspective, particularly in one's own, immediate life. We have a tendency to think in grandiose terms which, inevitably, means that we are rarely where we think we are in life. When we apply what is expected from us under our social contract and put ourselves under the figurative microscope, we see who we are and our place in society. We need to acknowledge that. No matter what that ends up being. Fortunately, acknowledgment does not mean acceptance; we live in a country where we are socially mobile, either upwards or downwards.

Certain words are capitalized throughout the text. This is not an attempt to personify those words but to give them a strict definition much as in the practice of legal documents. The same word can mean different things to different people. Denotation vs. connotation. Moreover, we—all of us and whether we are aware of it or not—attach emotional significance to words. The type and extent of those emotions are not consistent from person to person. Given the size and diversity of our society, it seemed prudent to standardize the meanings of frequently used words in the text as they relate to proffered concepts and idealizations.

Another quick note: Two references come from Christian publications: one by an Anglican apologetic; the other by a Roman Catholic Jesuit. The intent is not to convert anyone nor is it to imply that only Christians are capable of such insights. As the text makes clear, religion has no place in our social contract. Religion should remain personal, serving to help strengthen and guide a person in the practice of what is right. These references are merely more familiar to the author than others. Moreover, the ideas taken from those publications are not of a religious nature. Similar such observations have been or may have been noted in other religious or secular publications.

This work is a call to arms for America. It is likely to spur some agreement and some disagreement, but in the end if it spurs action, then it can be considered a success.

The Social Contract

Since humankind began measuring time, people voluntarily have come together and have lived under the umbrella of single systems. They do so for a number of reasons: common ancestry, common beliefs, common geography, common language, common goals, and security, to name a few. And when they do this, there is a tacit acknowledgment between the individuals that comprise the society as to what values define their group as a society. Oftentimes these values separate and make them distinct from other groups. There is also an unspoken understanding that the foremost responsibility of each member of the society is to maintain and uphold these values. This we call the Social Contract.

Some may argue that there are cultures in which its members are forced into a social system by an oligarchy, a dictator, a junta, clergy, or a caste system, and that this oppression of the masses offers no chance for social evolution. History tells us otherwise. What we see is that, in early societies, the weak congregate to the strong mainly for protection or fall victim to the strong for lack of it. Unchecked, the strong oftentimes prey on the weak, exploiting them for their own gain. When competition is introduced, a victor emerges controlling a certain area and subjects the surviving masses in exchange for his protection. Despite our present-day sensibilities, this is, nevertheless, a valid system—albeit a heavily biased one—and one that persists until that social unit decides to opt for another system. The Magna Carta, Tennis Court Rebellion, French Revolution, American Revolution, Meiji Restoration, and Russian Revolution demonstrate that history is replete with examples of how societies affected these changes and how social evolution—peacefully or otherwise—results in a new organism.

In recent history and in our particular case, we aren't required to sign a loyalty oath or some other legal document that spells out our duties and responsibilities to live in our society. In today's world that is as uncommon as a T-Rex. Yet by the time we are able to form our first words, we have an understanding of what kind of society in which we live, and, more or less, the values that make that society congeal to form a single, distinct system. In this sense, our environment—our society—forges how we live and in what fashion we interact with those around us. Simply put, we have an early and almost innate understanding of what is acceptable and unacceptable behavior in our particular system.

No society will remain perpetually *in situ*, particularly as progress and evolution abounds around them, rather it is reasonable to expect that some prevailing values will morph into new values. Sometimes this occurs over time;

sometimes it is a fractured change, but whether the former or the latter, it is, in an ideal society, done with the consent of the masses. In this process, it is also reasonable to expect that some members of a society will not agree to adopt whatever new values to which the majority gravitate, and so those members are faced with a choice: Conform to the new paradigm, or leave that society for another one. As these changes play out over time, the overarching hope is that a society will build upon the foundations laid for it by its predecessors and that they will evolve into a better, more advance people. The society should be converging on more and more common and centric values that represent the psyche of the masses as a whole rather than a slim margined majority. Where early changes may only be made with a simple majority, later changes should be approaching a super-majority.

The populating of America saw people who originally found themselves in societies that evolved in a manner that was contrary to their values and so opted to leave those for the opportunity of a new and different one. America was, to the Europeans, an uncharted and untainted land where a group of like-minded people could, more or less, establish a community with whatever rules they wanted. Even with the presence of the Native Americans, early America was rife in land providing for habitation in relative isolation. This provided the perfect blank canvas for disaffected groups from the Old World and to create societies more in line with their individual and respective ethos.

Soon, however, this influx of people, by their sheer numbers, closed the gaps between communities leading to a more unified society. We regard this unification and the changes that ensued as our national history. With the advent of the American Revolution, we, as a society, determined that a society framed without the will of the people was not an acceptable model in which liberty minded people could exist and prosper. Revolution, though, does not come without some type of consensus; an overwhelming consensus that focuses on a common thread. History books chronicle this rallying cry as a function of inadequate representation in government. And while the colonies fought for their freedom from England, they were not exactly fighting for a unified America. They wanted their own autonomy, free to create whatever systems best suited them and maintained with only a loose syndicate between other states. A Republic comprised of independent States. It took nearly a decade for the statesmen of the time to arrive at the flavor of democracy we practice today.

Framing a democracy that provides liberties for all and providing for its evolution over time sounds complicated and a bit overwhelming. Even knowing what we know today. Not so. If it appears complicated, it's because we are interjecting our emotion, biases, and desires in the mix; we are looking for a system specific to the one to be imposed on the many rather than *vice versa.* Yet, if we were to retrospectively summarize the impetus of our Revolution and the subsequent mores that are the foundation of our society, it would be this: Do what is right.

There will be an inevitable cacophony of objections: Who's to say what's right and what's wrong? Religion will inevitably enter that din, as will the *nature vs. nuture* argument. But we need to make something perfectly clear from the outset: A democracy only works IF the constituents, by and of themselves individually, understand what is Right and what is Wrong. Yes, Laws are necessary, but these are the stick to Right's carrot and only let us know what nastiness is in store for us if we opt to do Wrong. No set of Laws can cover the totality of person's actions or behavior from moment to moment. But here's the real essence: If we believe that we as a people don't know what is right from what is wrong, then someone needs to tell us. That mindset would serve to endorse Thomas Hobbes' "Leviathan" or alternatively titled, "The Matter, Forme, and Power of a Common-Wealth Ecclesiasticall and Civil," (Hobbes, 1651).

Hobbes was a 17th century English philosopher who was, arguably, the creator of the social contract theory which, simply put, stated that the individuals in a state surrender rights and freedoms to an authority in exchange for security and preservation of the society and its values. He went on to advocate that a single, all powerful sovereign was the cornerstone of a good government and that a sovereign should dictate what was right, what was wrong, what was acceptable, and what was unacceptable in a society. Hobbes dismissed democracy out of hand. If a man, elected into an assembly, was faced with an issue on which to deliberate, his private concerns would outweigh public concerns, and nature would dictate that he vote to preserve those private concerns. In other words, he would not necessarily do what is Right.

The skepticism still remains: Do we, innately, know what is Right and what is Wrong? There have been arguments about this going back at least as far as Aristotle who in his description of man as political animal asserts that man is distinct from other animals in that he alone has the perception of good and bad, and right and wrong. Voltaire, in all his brashness, recognized that this knowledge of right and wrong was independent of any dogma and was a concept the common man was well acquainted when he said, "I have no morals, but I am a very moral man." But perhaps the best and most concise explanation is offered by C.S. Lewis. In "The Law of Human Nature," the first chapter of his apologetic, "Mere Christianity" (Lewis, 1952), Lewis demonstrates in a very practical and laic fashion how we have an instinctive idea of what is Right and what is Wrong. He begins with how people quarrel, and, by listening to what they say, how we can gain insight into our grasp of Right and Wrong. When people quarrel, the cause is often that one person is not very happy with the behavior of another. Some possible comments could be: "How'd you like it if I did that to you," or "You promised," or "Why are you pushing me, I didn't do anything to you?" These types of comments suggest that the protagonist is holding the antagonist to a certain standard and that the antagonist is somehow violating that standard. The antagonist replies with what s/he believes is an exception to that standard. Both sides, perhaps without even knowing, are invoking fair play, and the fact that they start by quarreling and not physically fighting seems to suggest that each is appealing to this unwritten, ethereal law of nature to which they both tacitly agree. Moreover, we see this behavior in the educated and uneducated alike; in both children and adults.

Some may posit that culture defines the limits of Right and Wrong, but when we look at the ancient moralities of the Egyptians, Hindus, Greeks, Romans, Japanese, Chinese, and Celts, we may be surprised to see how very strikingly similar they are even though they developed independently of one another. In what society do we see that traitorous actions are rewarded or that you get a civic award for thievery? Is cowardice ever condoned? Or breaking promises ever lauded? No, we may find a person who says in one moment they don't believe in real Right and Wrong but will renege on that in the next. He may break his promise to you, but when you break yours to him, he'll complain that it's not fair. It's not Right.

Now there will be instances where certain individuals cannot grasp Right and Wrong. This is the way of nature. Just as we have albinos, color-blind people, or deaf people, there will be exceptions, but, by and large, it seems axiomatic that people know what is inherently Right and what is inherently Wrong.

At this point, it is important to agree on some recurring terminology. The reason for this is plain: Words, aside from their dictionary meanings, can carry emotional connotations, and these connotations are not always consistent from one person to another. The result of this disparity in any discourse is that our arguments may hinge on words that convey a different feeling to various involved parties only to find out in the end that they all have been in agreement the whole time.

When we speak of "Government," we are referring to an organization established by the entirety of the people, who we call the "Constituency," which cedes certain services and resources needed for the Government to fulfill its obligations to the Constituency. The "Republic" is a confederation of individually governed geographical areas we call "States." From a hierarchical perspective: The Government ensures homogeneity of the Social Contract across the Republic while the States allow for individual regional and cultural differences to that contract to the extent that those differences do not contradict the Government.

The notion of Constituency is separated into two parts: A Contributing Constituency and a Non-Contributing Constituency. The former refers to those individuals in the Republic who are meeting their obligations under the Social Contract; the latter to those who are not. Those obligations are measured in terms of both the Republic and the State. They are not mutually exclusive; that is, one cannot be considered a Contributing Constituent if he meets his obligations to the State but not the Republic, or *vice versa*. To reside in a State is to reside in the Republic. One cannot reside in the Republic without residing in a State. In terms of those Constituency who, from time to time and temporarily, reside in a foreign entity outside the Republic and has no obligations to a State, their obligations must be met to the Republic as the Republic may require for individuals in those circumstances, from time to time, so that they may still be considered as part of the Contributing Constituency.

One pillar of a good Society is Reason and the Reasonableness of its Constituency in the sense that Reason is a process by which a suitable outcome to a problem is determined based on weighing elements of that problem against possible solutions while simultaneously being detached from the problem. When we Reason in mathematics, we are agonistic to the solution. We are, however, concerned with an appropriate methodology to arrive at an answer. When we are comfortable with the algorithm, we accept that the answer is correct whether that answer was what we expected or not. And then we move on to the next problem. Nothing in this reasoning has anything to do with any attachment, sentiment, or feelings we may harbor to either the problem, the methodology, or the solution. It is quite simply cold, hard math.

Unfortunately, social problems are not quite so easily solved. While we must strive to Reason, we need to also consider softer, almost undefinable elements that pervade most situations. In this, it is important to distinguish between Emotion and Compassion. The former creates chasms between people, fuels anger and hate, and—if allowed to dominate our Society—will lead the Republic into an abyss from which there may be no return. The latter allows for the measured and balanced consideration of a particular situation given the circumstances unique to that situation and in the context of what the Society has deemed to be fair. While Emotion equates to an almost instinctive, *id*-like response, Compassion is a delicate balance between emotion, empathy, and reason. Prudent and thoughtful use of Compassion leads to unity and justice; rampant and frequent use of Emotion leads to division and anarchy.

The terms and conditions of the American Social Contract are really quite simple. We have agreed that we have the opportunity to pursue any course of action and any form of living insofar as these pursuits and courses of action do not infringe on the ability of others to pursue their respective courses of action and forms of living. In this regard, we ought to form only the minimum number of Laws whereby each member is required to be familiar with these Laws with the expectation that any breach of these Laws—whether intentional or incidental—remain at a minimum. At the core of our contract also lies the liberty that is commensurate with these pursuits and the freedom from wrongful or arbitrary prosecution of the rights granted by the Society. We also enjoy the ability to control the direction the Society takes by directing representation in whatever Government serves the Society from time to time.

To enable this contract, we collectively decided to form a constitutional and representative Government. That Government is divided into three separate but intertwined parts: The Executive, the Legislative, and the Judiciary. The Executive are enforcers of laws and provides the general policies of leadership; the Legislative makes laws and approves use of Government resources; and the Judiciary decides the right and just enactment, interpretation, and enforcement of the rights, laws, and policies determined by the other two parts. None can operate independently or in a void of the other, and the successful administration of the Government relies on these three working in concert. We, as the Constituency, must understand and—more importantly—respect each in its duties and obligations to the Republic or the State, as the case may be. In this fashion, when conflict or contentious issues arise and as we work collaboratively for a resolution, we know where and when to focus our efforts in that process.

Blaming the Executive branch for enforcing laws passed by the Legislative and approved by the Judiciary is a waste of our time and merely serves to prolong a solution while needlessly inflaming parts of the Constituency. Likewise, lambasting Legislators for the misinterpretation or poor execution of their legislation is misdirected energy. No man nor group of men possess omnipotence. It is not reasonable to expect that we can completely anticipate every possible future scenario when crafting Government. What is reasonable is to expect that each branch does what is Right and what is good for the Republic (or the State) in the context of their respective mandates.

Our obligations to Government and its to us are also quite simple. As a people, we agree to enable and empower the Government through monetary contribution, certain resources, and service. In return the Government pledges us safety, security, and infrastructure. Anything beyond this is superfluous, confounding, and risks choking our liberties and pursuits imagined under the Social Contract. Moreover, powers exerted or assumed by the Government in excess of these can fragment the Society into groups who endeavor to manipulate

Government into giving preeminence to their particular group at the expense of remaining Constituency.

The danger lies with believing that: (i) we are free in the absolute sense; and (ii) freedom is free. At the heart of any social contract is the principle that one gets nothing for free. Happiness is not something that we achieve by breathing the air; it something we work hard to attain. If it were not hard won, it would lose its luster, and its value—as with everything in abundance—would diminish. With this in mind, we can succinctly outline what we, as the Constituents, owe the Government. We finance the execution of the Government through taxes which ought to be fairly levied. We provide service by donating some portion of our lives which ought to be in consideration of our abilities and from which service we receive recompense to sustain our lives for that period. We are responsible for diligently searching, identifying, and providing the Government with duly elected representatives who are qualified to conduct the business of Government. When we meet these criteria, we can be called Contributing Constituents. If we are not meeting these criteria, we have breached our fiduciary responsibilities under the Social Contract and, as a result, are a burden on the Society.

In return for our taxes and service, Government ought to provide us with safety for all its members which includes, but is not limited to, protection from crime and wrongdoing by our fellow Americans; protection from (to the extent that the society deems it practicable) acts of God; personal safety within the environment of the Society; responsible and safe conduct of corporations, employers, and the government as well as any product or by product thereof; an infrastructure that is well maintained and current in its know-how, construction, and components; systems that provide confidence for investments and purchases; and a system that allows for the fair election and oversight of Government representatives.

Additionally, Government is obliged to offer security which includes, but is not limited to, a standing military for protection against foreign threats; Laws to determine the rights and criteria of Society with such laws being representative and commensurate with the ideals and the will of the Contributing Constituency as it exists from time to time; mechanisms to prosecute injustice and receive compensation for wrongs under the law; and the ability to undertake the pursuit of or avail oneself to anything in Society so long as it is lawful and does not infringe upon the liberty of others.

To facilitate the multi-variegated pursuits of Society, Government is also compelled to provide and maintain a modern infrastructure where such infrastructure serves to propel Society forward both in technology and in its social evolution.

Our Social Contract stands as the foundation upon which all else is built. It is the single thing around which we can all collectively rally. It is the crutch to lean upon when certain reforms seem unbearable. It is the glue that holds us together as a Union whether we be Democrat, Republican, or Other. It is our national identity and what intertwines us. The issue, it seems today, is one of mission drift. Whether this is a result of design or deference, it appears that very few acknowledge or have an understanding of our Social Contract—if they even know it exists at all. Taken as a whole, the nation's Social Contract looks more like shattered glass than a solid pane through which would allow us to see all things clearly. Such a fragmented and fractured social contract will not nearly be robust enough to withstand the hard road we necessarily must go down to ensure the survivability of America in these modern times.

Fair and Right

Understanding what is fair is the beginning of knowing right action. Intuitively, we understand what is fair although we always seem to be much better discerning that in situations in which we are not involved. While we are conscionable enough to admit that we always want what is fair for everyone, it can be a battle when a specific outcome affects us as individuals. Our human nature is such that we provide as much as we can for ourselves with little or no regard for others. To our credit, we acknowledge this, and throughout our history have tried to implement systems that help remove this bias. This has been accomplished by setting down, in writing and through actions by duly elected representatives, standards by which fair can be measured. We call these fair standards Laws.

Fair, for such a small word, can be a complicated concept and is worth exploring so that we might better have an idea of how we arrive at it, how we apply it, and how we need to accept it. From this basic understanding we can erect, block by block, a solid and reasonable structure that serves the entirety of Society in the form of Law from which we have a platform which advantages us in determining what is Right.

Let's start with the basest of examples of comparing fair and right: Necessities for personal survival. There are three people and three loaves of bread. Fair is giving each person one loaf. Right is giving more to the person who is hungriest. A simple situation with a relatively straightforward solution.

A bit more complicated example is one which may be more familiar. There are three people and three boxes. These three people want to watch a baseball game over a fence. Fair is giving each person one box. Right is giving boxes to those who need them to see over the fence.

The examples given thus far have dealt with material items; discerning what is fair is far more complicated as we rarely deal with just physical things like loaves of bread or boxes. We need to be able to apply the concept of fair over two realms: The tangible and the intangible. At this stage in our Society's evolution, we see the results of how our predecessors distinguished between the two, what problems occur in how fair is defined in each instance, and what solutions they rendered to accommodate Society. What we don't see are the intricacies in that process. An overview of that would, perhaps, give us an appreciation for the results we see as well as aid us in applying fair in whatever situation we may find ourselves.

In terms of the tangible realm and simply put: Fairness is an empirical concept based largely on pure mathematics. It relies on something being defined in terms of the countable and the divisible. It does not need to take into account any other elements. You simply divide the number of recipients into the quantities to be distributed, and you have what is fair. If there are three boxes and three people, then fair is one box per person. Each person receives an equal portion without regard to their sex, religion, hair color, height, ethnicity, or need. There is an absence of Emotional interpretation.

Fair, in this sense, is easiest determined when the items to be distributed are equally divisible by the number of recipients. This, however, is almost never the case. What if, in our example of boxes and people at the ballgame, there are two boxes and three people? Division dictates that each person receive two-thirds of a box. That would be fair. It is not, however, practical since the box would no longer be a box and therefore has lost whatever intrinsic value that made it useful. In this case, when we rely on division of items over number of recipients, the concept of fair fails.

To achieve the objective and to ensure that the boxes retain their initial value—that is, they must remain intact—we need to employ a system of "sharing." Each person gets the use of a box temporarily, and when a certain predetermined time has elapsed, that person passes the use of the box to the next person. In our example and over a period of one hour, one person can have access to a box for forty minutes.

When the boxes are used to watch the ballgame, all things being equal, each person can watch forty minutes of the game per hour while standing on a box. Of course, if we introduce the variable of height, that may no longer be true. Should one of the individuals be tall enough to see over the fence, that individual can watch the entire game without the need of the box. For two-thirds of each hour, that individual will have the option to stand on a box or not stand on the box. Perhaps standing on the box allows him to see the game better than the other two individuals. Either way, he will be able to watch the entire game. An individual not tall enough to see over the fence unaided can only see the game for two-thirds of each hour.

In terms of watching the game, the shorter person is disadvantaged, and should we apply a fair standard to "watching the game," it would be unfair. But we are looking at the use of boxes, and so as a tangible asset we need to disregard anything that is not countable or divisible. To assert that the shorter person should have exclusive, or more exclusive, use of the box would require the division of the boxes to be made biasedly, in this case according to height. This would imply that the division of the boxes is predicate upon a specific purpose and not simply because they are boxes. The assumption is that they will be used exclusively as enablers to watch the ballgame and have no other function. But boxes can have a variety of purposes, and different individuals may employ boxes in different ways. In this instance, "fair" would not depend on the use of the box, simply the number. A short person may use it to look over the fence at the ball game while the tall person may opt to sit on it.

The most noticeable consequence of fair with regard to tangibles is that of ownership. To divide two boxes among three people would indicate that no one person would have exclusive, sole ownership over one box. This introduces the idea of community property. Since the ownership is transferred every two-thirds of a time period, the temporal owner is not at liberty to dispose of the box as he sees fit. The box cannot be altered or destroyed or committed to a third party beyond its ability to be passed onto a different temporal possessor in its original state and at the appointed time.

What is described here is theoretical socialism. In order for the box to be transferred from one temporal owner to another, it must remain in a system that allows and provides for this transference. Necessarily, that system would be comprised of the individuals to which the boxes were distributed. Because each member of that system has a vested interested in ensuring the integrity of the boxes, that is, their quality and serviceability, the system would be self-policing. At any given time, the temporal, non-possessing members would be providing oversight to the temporal, possessing members. In this fashion the temporal, non-possessing members would have a greater assurance that when they became temporal, possessing members the boxes would enter their temporal possession in the same state as when they entered the possession of former temporal, possessing members.

But what if the tangible item is disposable; that is, it can only be used once and then is depleted, destroyed, or otherwise rendered in a state less than its original state? Upon considering disposable tangibles, as long as they can be evenly divisible among the members of the system, there can be no doubt as to what is fair. On the other hand, if it occurs that those items are prevalent in a number less than the members of the system—let's use the example of the rare and highly coveted Chateau Lafite Rothschild wine where only a very small and limited number exist—then fair division renders the property unusable. In such a case, we encounter a hurdle to being materially fair. In such cases, the obvious solution is that no one in the system is granted use of this property. There would be no owners and the disposable tangibles would need to lie outside the system.

Unfortunately, this makes these items of no value, and there would be no motivation to produce them. This, however, is not practical in a society and does not translate into real life. Many materials, by their very nature, are disposable and occur at numbers less than the applicable populace or in amounts that render the division of such items useless. In our Society, we solve this problem by assigning a value to such items often using currency standards. That value is generally a result of supply and demand and what the market can bear for such items. The scarcer an item and the more it is needed by the citizenry, the more value it has. Conversely, the more abundant an item and the need by the citizenry not so great, the less value it has. Oversimplified economics.

This has been a bit of an excruciating detailed-laden process, but what we have arrived at is the idea of fair ownership of Property, where Property is the exclusive, private ownership of tangible items. It is important we understand how this works in our Society and, more importantly, that we accept it as part of our Society. There can sometimes be a tendency in a free market society where social evolution finds itself in a place where some individuals believe that it is unfair that other individuals have more Property than they. These disaffected individuals allege that they, too, should have the same or equivalent Property, and are, in fact, deserving of it. This likely stems from feelings of inadequacy. In our Society, the amount of Property one has is a direct reflection of the decisions an individual makes *vis-à-vis* priorities in quality and/or quantity of living and in committing an amount of an individual's worth to Property. When we say "worth' we say it in the quantitative sense, not the qualitative. In general, everyone in our Society has the same access to Property; however, not everyone has the same ability to obtain Property. This lies with the individual and not with how we have established fair access to Property.

It falls to each individual in a society to determine how relevant an item is to their existence and to prioritize, from their own resources, which Properties take precedence over others. In perfect socialism, every citizen has the same limited monetary resources making the opting for particular properties a double-edged sword: To obtain what an individual believes is necessary or desired, other Properties must be sacrificed.

Unfortunately, the practice of pure socialism has not proven to be a historically successful model for humankind. With whatever altruistic intentions we may start, we seem to have had difficulties in reigning in our Emotion over Reason, and in that never-ending battle—no matter what the social structure—our basic nature dictates that we gravitate toward the self-centric. We want self-gratification, and part of that is believing no one can have more than we. We revel in things we have that our neighbors do not, using this a measure of superior self-worth while cursing our neighbors for having what we do not, complaining it's not "fair" and feeling inferior and left behind. Few of us are happy with what we have.

The accumulation of Property then becomes a function of one's ability to pay for that Property. Each individual must make their own decisions as to what Property s/he requires or desires for their own, unique lifestyles in the context of their ability to acquire and maintain that Property. Not everyone's financial means are the same, nor is there a fixed lifestyle to which all in Society aspire, so comparing what Property one individual has to the Property another has would be senseless. No two situations are the same. As difficult as it may be, we need to resist the urge to use such comparisons as a measure of a happy existence.

The core to fairness in Property is an amalgamation of sufficiency and contentment. What is enough? What is appropriate? When is satisfaction met? Applying some self-awareness to our individual situations can lead us to an answer that would steer us away from opulence and leave us with, surprisingly, a fraction of the Property we have now and with a greater quality of life.

Now when we speak of fair in terms of intangibles, what is fair and unfair is determined by a consensus of a society through whatever mechanism it has provided for such deliberations. Laws, regulations, various types of standards, judicial remedies, and legal processes can all be considered intangibles. The theoretical bars for "fair" are, once again, immutable and without appeal. They must be applied evenly in every instance to all members of a society without exception.

On a theoretical level, this all seems to make perfectly good sense. To apply a standard in one case and ignore it in another would be illogical and a contradiction to its entire *raison d'etre*—that is: To be fair. Yet when we start dealing with specific cases—particularly those involving ourselves—suddenly we all have our own interpretation of how and when to apply those standards of fairness. Let's take speed limits. The interstate speed limit in most states is posted at 65 mph. That number was not arrived at by throwing darts at a board and adding up the score. There was a process, through duly appointed committees, involving several hearings from which a recommendation was given to duly elected officials for deliberation and a vote leading to a definitive number. So, is it fair that anyone traveling in excess of 65 mph be cited for speeding? The answer is, of course, "yes." When the State choses to enforce this fairness standard randomly, or when it more often chooses another arbitrary number at which it will cite speeding drivers, the concept of fair has been discarded for expedience. A driver sees a plethora of other drivers sailing down the highway at speeds in excess of 75 mph, sometimes right past law enforcement vehicles. That driver reasons that since law enforcement permits this speed limit rather than a standard, the posted speed limit signs must be more of a recommendation—at least in this particular stretch of highway. Seconds later after speeding up to stay with traffic he is pulled over and cited for speeding. Fair?

Absolutely not. Every single driver speeding should be ticketed. What lies at the heart of this, though, is the scale of enforceability at this point in time. If tomorrow, the police were to begin strict enforcement of this Law, there wouldn't be enough officers to issue tickets. If we employed radar cameras on overpasses, tens of millions of people would lose their license in a single day. Perhaps all drivers. Absent a huge reboot in our mindset, it is unlikely that our behavior will align with Society's standards when we know we can already exceed those standards with few—if any—consequences. This doesn't deter from what is fair to Society as a whole. In our example of speeding, the limits are clearly posted so we have no excuse when we are cited for going too fast. We wrongly think it unfair as we watch a myriad of other drivers elude a ticket when, in fact, we need to be aware that when we break this—or any fairness standard—we enter a pool where we are all knowingly breaking a Law and are leaving consequence to chance.

But fair is something we need to take seriously, and we need to be ever vigilante that we don't drift away from established standards unless those changes are preceded by proper legislation. Doing so only serves to create divisions—real or perceived—between the uneven application of those standards. Firstly, there may be no apparent underlying reason for such incongruous enforcement. But, as the saying goes, nature abhors a vacuum. Where no reason exists, one will be fabricated. And those reasons will, inevitably, be touchstone ones: religion, race, gender, and age. Anything to invoke an Emotional response in the public. Nothing good ever comes of that. The reaction on the one side will be that of victimization and on the other righteous indignation. Secondly, we risk falling into the trap of justifying our bad behavior by the bad behavior of others. The foundation of our Social Contract is to do what is Right. This is easily achieved when everyone around us is doing the right thing and is easiest to do when we are on display. But when we find ourselves in a situation where the herd is breaking bad, we need to resist the urge to exercise that herd mentality and, instead, do what is Right. Surprisingly, that too, can be as infectious as doing what is Wrong.

Fair is the progenitor of Right. In our Society, fair is the result of mutually agreed upon standards and practices all of which we, as individuals, acknowledge and by which we consent to abide as members of Society. When codified, we call them Laws. Laws can be referenced and enforced. They are immutable; that is, they are ideally applied evenly over every situation and not open to interpretation based on the circumstances of a situation. Laws are cold, hard and cruel; they are devoid of any emotion, particularly Compassion. Laws, in and of themselves, do not define what is Right in any situation, but only provide a rod by which we can begin to measure what is Right.

Any situation where Laws need to be applied is rarely a simple one and those situations almost never have a binary outcome. Most times there are circumstances surrounding the incident—whether for better or worse—that influence how and to what extent a Law was violated or to what extent it should be applied. In this we must distinguish between what is fair and what is just. The service of justice is an attempt to do what is Right. In that pursuit, we need to exercise Compassion which Compassion is applied to both the violator of the Law and any affected third party. What we need to avoid is the introduction of Emotion. When we become overwhelmed with Emotion, it distorts our judgement, drives us away from right action, and leads to a disproportionate dispensation of punitive actions.

To assist us in Compassionate deliberations, we elect or have appointed judges in who we expect to be knowledgeable, reasonable, and consistent in their consideration of each different and unique case. As with any other Government official, we are not in search of a man-with-no-sin, but rather we are searching for persons who have demonstrated the ability to profit from experiences—both theirs and others, who can leverage those experiences to the best execution of their duties, and who are, naturally, familiar with Laws. As one would expect, we generally find these qualities in professionals, in people who have, more or less, dedicated their lives to ensuring right outcomes in what sometimes can be complicated and convoluted situations. Moreover, these judges need to reflect Society's current values and not necessarily those of the past. As a Society, it is our hope—our expectation—that each generation advances in values bringing us that much closer to the goal where each person in Society does what is Right without the need to enact and enforce more Laws to ensure such right action.

What has recently and often disrupted the right exercise of justice is when the case is first tried in the court of public opinion which court is overseen by a jury of Emotional extremists spurred on by the Fourth Estate. Sensationalism is a quick and cheap way to attract attention. In our Society where we believe that Government is required to provide evidence of guilt, such sensationalism is irresponsible. Any accused should be able to expect a trial by their peers where such peers make a determination of guilt or innocence by the Reasonable interpretation of evidence. With biased commentary that more and more presages a judicial proceeding, it becomes increasingly more difficult to ensure a trial in which the deliberators of that trial have not been influenced *a priori*.

There are several downstream effects of this "pre-trial" effect not the least of which are increased defense costs, pressure on the judiciary to levy severe and wrongful penalties, and—in the event of a "not guilty" verdict—the ruination of Reputation and bankruptcy of the defendant. In our pursuit of what is Right in this context—that is justice—Society ought to be equally prepared for verdicts that run in either direction and with equal commitment. Our plaintiffs and prosecutors need more of a Damocles Sword as they determine what to pursue *vis-à-vis* what cases can be successfully prosecuted. A defendant who spends months in prison and spends every cent they have on a defense and is, in the end, found innocent needs recompense from the plaintiff or prosecutors for wrongful prosecution. Compensation for damages suffered with respect to a defendant's Reputation need to include contributions from culpable members of the Fourth Estate.

The totality of this amount will, naturally, be an overwhelming figure but a necessary one. It is not enough to apologize and say "Sorry." Without other more concrete and meaningful gestures, these are just empty words used to make a bad and embarrassing situation go away. As in everyday situations, if anyone is truly sorry, they will do whatever it takes to make it right.

An unsettling trend we seem to be experiencing in our Society is pulling events from the distant past and trying them in a present-day court. While it never serves a Society to have wrongful behavior go unaddressed, it can be equally detrimental to justice in reviving or bringing to light long past events for the first time without irrefutable forensic evidence. In our Society, we have incorporated the concept of statutes of limitations which is meant to minimize these incidences. These statutes provide for a specific amount of time whereby a case may be made based on the date when the crime occurred. With very few exceptions, these limitations should govern the entirety of what venues our judiciary entertains.

It is essential we understand what these statutes do and how they impact our liberties and, more importantly, our freedoms. Without them, we may find ourselves in a situation where facts and truth may not determine either. For civil cases, "Statutes of limitation...are designed to promote justice by preventing surprises through the revival of claims that have been allowed to slumber until evidence has been lost, memories are faded, and witnesses have disappeared" (*Order of R.R. Telegraphers v. Railway Express Agency*, 321 US 342, 348-49, 64 S. Ct. 582,586, 1944). With respect to criminal cases, the purpose is to "limit exposure to criminal prosecution…to protect individuals against charges when the basic facts have become obscured by the passage of time and to minimize the danger of official punishment because of acts in the far-distant past" (*Toussle v. US*, 1970). Two factors immediately catch our attention: The passage of time as it impacts recollection and, more critically, the ability of the evidence to remain robust enough for a conviction. Historically, many distant past cases have relied on eyewitness testimony. Technological advances have provided us with better and more accurate forensic analytical methods which, if nothing else, has taught us that eyewitness testimony is unreliable at best. Psychologically, such testimony is subject to unconscious editing that can incorporate biases. In their January 1, 2010 article in the Scientific American, Arkowitz and Lilienfeld cited that 73% of 239 cases that were overturned by DNA evidence were conviction based on eyewitness testimony—two thirds of that having two or more eyewitnesses. And these cases were prosecuted in a timely fashion without the further influence of a passing of time. The definition of statute of limitations acknowledges that memories fade and realizes that we can unconsciously develop a revisionist history of our experiences from the past. This can be a barrier to a Right judgement.

We do not, in our Society, provide a statute of limitations for every violation of our Laws. This has, unfortunately, led to some civil cases being tried decades after the claim accrued or after the committing of the alleged criminal act. This inevitably leads to two issues in rendering a right decision. The first is, of course, the bar of evidence. Many recent cases have relied heavily on eyewitness testimony. We should all be self-aware enough to admit to forgetting things in our past; particularly, things to which we assigned no significant importance, or to which, at the time, did not set themselves apart from the context of the time. The second is the dismissal of the then fair standards and commonly and socially acceptable values in favor of applying current fair standards and values to an incident in the past. With the passage of time comes new information, changes in socially acceptable behavior, changes to fair standards, and changes in how we view the past. We cannot, in good conscience, discount what effect these have in how we remember or how we interpret a situation.

One of the singularly dangerous things a Society can do is spend its time critiquing the behavior and values of past generations using today's mores as a measuring stick. Aside from setting ourselves up for the same judgement years in the future, it ignores the progress in values and behavior made in Society—a progress we would expect to be making as an evolving society. There is a reason the rearview mirror in a car is smaller than the windshield: It is more important to see where we're going rather than focusing on where we've been. While it is true that those who fail to learn from history are doomed to repeat it (Santayana, 1905), those who fixate on the past have no future. Without any incorruptible forensic evidence, reliving tragedies from our past and stirring up specters of injustice with the intention of prosecuting them in the present-day serve no purpose other than to gain some self-satisfaction—either through the ruination of someone's Reputation made easy by the Fourth Estate or through some monetary settlement. Both result in an overloading of our justice system.

We do not wish to downplay or shrug off tragedies of the past that were not justly resolved nor do we submit that these tragedies should not be reviewed more than once under the constraints of the statutes of limitations determined by our duly elected officials; however, we are still a Society where a defendant is innocent until proven guilty, and in this present-day, hearsay is not evidence enough to convict—at least in a court. We see a different bar of evidence in the media, one which makes the selection of an unbiased jury, absent a dramatic change in venue, virtually impossible. There will always be an uncomfortable balance between the guilty set free and the innocent imprisoned, but we don't need to make that more difficult than it already is by allowing opinions, conjectures, second-hand information, and unreliable evidence to influence the process. Perhaps it would avail us in our endeavors to mute the cacophony of these forays by exercising a bit of empathy; that is, put ourselves in the position of any defendant, try to determine whether third party factors place the onus of evidence on the defendant to prove innocence or the prosecutors to prove guilt, and understand if we need to adjust our perception of the situation in order to provide the defendant the same degree of consideration which we would, ourselves, expect in the same circumstances.

In the end, the goal is to do what is Right. Not an easy thing. From our understanding of the distinction between fair and Right, we have made Laws to set the expectation of fair in both the tangible and intangible realms and that those Laws serve as the foundation of justice. Through our appointment or election of judges to interpret the application of those Laws on a case-by-case basis we can expect an unbiased determination of guilt, oftentimes through a jury of our peers. To realize all these things, we need to keep Emotion out of the equation, as difficult as that may be, and use our Compassion. To remain true to the pursuit of justice—that is, to do what is Right—is a testimony to the dedication we have in preserving our Society, a reaffirmation of our Social Contract, and—most importantly—a clear indicator of our continued progress into a more evolved, more perfect human race.

On Responsibility

In an undeveloped, unevolved society, status is measured by wealth, material possessions, and how much influence one has in affecting changes in a varying degree of circumstances. Most times, this status is at the expense of others. For magnates to do well, others have to do poorly. The underlying value of that kind of society is a focus on a "life of quantity" and not a "life of quality." In the instances where the rise of the few causes the decimation of the many, government is often called upon to intervene and reign in the destruction being wrought on society. They hold these czars accountable and, because these plutocrats lack the self-motivation born of moral integrity, force them kicking and screaming into a certain decorum of responsibility.

In contrast, status in an evolved society is measured by how well one faithfully executes duties according to one's responsibilities rather than by how much material or financial gains one amasses. Being diligent in one's responsibilities becomes society's expectation for each of its members. Outside of government, the degree of responsibility one possesses can often be a combination of one's material abundance and one's sphere of influence. To the extent that one can control events and outcomes within one's sphere of influence we call Power; the more control, the more Power. Power demands responsibility. To paraphrase the late, great Stan Lee, "With great power comes great responsibility."

Power takes many forms and depends on one's sphere of influence. An individual's basic sphere of influence is at arm's length, literally and figuratively. It contains those people and things in one's life that have an impact on one's prosperity and those people and things on which one can affect change thereby influencing their prosperity. This sphere gradually radiates out farther and farther as one becomes more and more successful and proficient in the management and application of Power. Rarely can this be managed without Reputation, with Reputation being the qualities of an individual—whether for good or bad—as perceived by those within that individual's sphere of influence.

There is a notion that the only thing that a person truly owns is Reputation. All else is transient. We don't own our homes; fail to pay your property taxes and see what happens. Our clothes are bought, worn, and discarded when they become unserviceable. Material things come and go in our lives with all too much regularity. The only thing that seems to persist the entirety of our lives is our Reputation; that is, how people perceive us. It's the only thing you can take with you. It is the only thing that survives the grave. It lasts for as long as we are remembered. For good or bad.

We do not, of our accord, weave this mantle and wear it as we please. Neither do we shop for it or have it manufactured to a set of specifications. Some small part of it comes from how we would like to be perceived, but nearly all of it comes from our behavior. It's not what we think or who we think we are, but what we do. How we act. Consistency. Honesty. Integrity. Morale courage. Use of Power. These are a few of the measuring sticks we employ as we develop opinions of others and others on us which contribute to the forging of Reputations. And we should have a very keen and active interest in forging our Reputations. They dictate possibilities.

Some would argue that it doesn't matter what other people think of you, it's what you think of yourself that matters. That sounds good. Sounds positive. Sounds encouraging. Great for self-confidence. But this is tantamount to saying that Reputation counts for nothing. Your actions mean nothing. Reality is swept under the carpet. Too many times we hear this advice doled out to those who fare poorly in integrating themselves into Society. It serves to assuage those who are having trouble meeting life head on, or for those who lack the strength of character to overcome problems as they inevitably arise from time to time, or for those who unsuccessfully try to extend beyond their own sphere of influence. Whatever the intention and whatever the circumstance, this advice ignores the fact that, by being an integral part of any society, a person exists and prospers at the hands of other members of that society. It matters a great deal what people think of you and who they believe you are. Reputation is the fuel that propels us through life. Its strength confers Power on us and widens our spheres of influence.

This would be a good point to address the myth that often accompanies "It doesn't matter what people think of you," which is the invariable, "You can be whatever you want to be if you set your mind to it." Other than being part a locker room motivational speech, this is clearly absolute nonsense. A paraplegic will never be the starting quarterback for the New England Patriots no matter how much he sets his mind to it. We, individually, possess varying strengths and weaknesses that make us either suitable or unsuitable, as the case may be, for certain tasks. We can only be the best possible versions of ourselves. And to this end we must, needs be, set our minds completely, utterly, and without reservation towards that end. Along the way, we need frequent and healthy doses of self-awareness to determine how, where, and to what extent to best apply the particular qualities and talents we possess. We need the presence of mind to distinguish between the difficult to obtain dreams from the impossible to obtain dreams if we are to best use the resources at our disposal—particularly, the resource of time.

Reputation is in a constant state of flux; we are being judged at every turn. The quality of our lives directly depends on those judgements. The university we attend, jobs we get, promotions or raises that come our way, husbands and wives we take, and friends we have, are all a result of how well others perceive the values we successfully project. If the common values held in esteem in our Society serve as the cauldron in the making of a

Reputation, Trust is the litmus paper by which the quality of that brew is tested. Trust is the belief that a person's Reputation remains consistent, is without guile, and is resilient. Trust is hard won but easily lost. "One 'oh shit' erases ten 'atta boys'." Crude, but true. A hiccup in behavior that is contrary to a person's Reputation and violates Society's Trust is met with immediate and detrimental consequences the extent of which depends on the severity of the breach and the strength of Reputation. To regain Trust oftentimes requires an uphill battle where behavior is continually measured against the former state of Reputation until there becomes enough data to be confident that the earlier hiccup was an outlier. Unfortunately, there is no set formula for this recovery, and it often differs from case to case, person to person even with all other things being equal. As members of Society we have two overarching obligations in this: On the one side to be as diligent as possible in maintaining, safeguarding, and improving our Reputations; and on the other side to use Compassion when someone's Trust falters.

Responsibility starts with ourselves. Before we can move outward from our basic sphere of influence, we need to be able to handle ourselves. No one is going to put Trust into someone who can't manage their own affairs no matter how competent that person may appear. We need to be responsible for our lifestyle and not exceed a standard of living that will present some future burden on Society or cause us to self-destruct. How we live our individual lives boils down to our wages and benefits and the decisions we make concerning their disposition. Of the two, wages determine the quantity of life we can lead. Wages determine the house in which we live, the car which we drive, the clothes which we wear, the fun we can have. In short, it defines our standard of living. Rationale spending of wages helps to ensure our needs are met and that we might have the best quality of life obtainable. Unfortunately, and all too often, Emotion usurps Reason so that spending becomes an issue that threatens the existence of the individual and presents a burden that may need to be borne by the rest of Society.

The American dream: Two cars in the drive, a boat, a swimming pool in the backyard, split ranch house, vacation trips every year, and more disposable income than my neighbor. Possible. But not always. Society has brought itself to the brink of financial ruin a number of times in recent memory because this dream, like a demon, has possessed too many of our people who aren't in a position to achieve it. They bankrupt themselves trying. They tax the resources of Society by trying. And it isn't the trying that is necessarily wrong; it's either the not accepting or not understanding where they inhabit in the socio-economic strata or the need to amplify their self-worth through material accumulations. But this self-inflicted devastation is preventable. Easily. It's simple math. Addition and subtraction. By taking a bit of time and running through the pluses and minuses faced every month, one can quickly arrive at how much disposable income is on hand. From that, they can decide how to appropriate it. Budgets are easy and Emotionless. They speak the truth—sometimes a truth we don't want to hear—but a truth nevertheless. If the numbers don't add up, then there's a problem. If we don't fix that problem, then all the European vacations and all the cars and the boats and the swimming pool and the house will not compensate for the hardships we will need to endure in order to right that ship.

Human nature combined with the richness of our Society are the enemies in our efforts to settle into a rational lifestyle. In our Society, we have long since stopped battling every minute of every day for survival. We live lives of comparative ease—even when we look at other first world nations. We look for things to occupy our free time; we look for enjoyment. The quest, though, seems to be insatiable. Like a broken record, all we seem to say is "more, more, more." What is missing is contentment. Not necessarily getting what we want, but wanting what we have. Human nature contains no small amount of jealousy. We see things we don't have. We see others happy with them. We want that happiness. We believe that having whatever others have will be the thing to finally make us happy. It may provide some satisfaction for a while, but inevitably, it doesn't fill the emptiness that envy always brings, and we find ourselves forever disappointed. And we find our attics, basements, and garages full. It makes one wonder how much all these disappointments have cost us over the long term.

The challenge to personal Responsibility, then, is to summon the strength of character that provides stewardship over the use of one's resources, resist impetuous urges to satisfy transient wants, ignore the alleged greener grass on the other side of the fence, and be content knowing one is leading as rich a life as one can under the circumstances.

There are members of our Society who have continued to amass Power to the point where they are Responsible for the lives and well-being of other Constituents. Employers, large and small, are such members. Clergymen are others. Leaders in Government, unions, and professional associations still others. In many instances the degree of influence they wield is uncontestable and permanent. They undertake and oversee activities in Society that demand a decorum of Compassion in the exercise of their Power as it affects the people in their sphere of influence. The well-being of those individuals is as integral to a sustainable business model as being profitable. Engaging in business practices that marginalize or exploit employees in favor of personal gain—be it wealth or position—is irresponsible, and such conduct has no place in our Society.

The tragedy we have experienced is that rather than to embrace this kind of Responsibility, we have a growing trend that skews in the complete opposite direction; that is, one that favors the sacrificing of our neighbor upon the altar of greed to appease the god of Money, all in hopes of being a beneficiary to the promises of influence, power, and material goods that this false god offers. Employers have become more and more anesthetized towards the plight of those upon whose backs they achieve their wealth and power, and focus solely on climbing a ladder they believe leads to a kind of heaven that sets them above the Social Contract which, ironically, has provided the rungs upon which they scale.

In an attempt to stop this downward spiral into despotism, and to fulfill its obligation under the Social Contact to provide safety and security, the Government, over time, has been forced to enact an overwhelming plethora of standards protecting Society from exploitation. Unfortunately, try as they may, Government cannot plug all the holes, and the greedy continue to frustrate Society as a whole. So, while the problem persists, we are continually inundated by more and more regulations which can sometimes deter responsible people from pursuing opportunities that would otherwise benefit Society. It is too convoluted. Bureaucracies reign where the simplest of solutions is needed: Do what is Right.

The weight of any social pyramid rests on its foundation. Without that foundation, the pyramid topples into a pile of stones. Ensuring that the foundation remains strong and well-cared for ensures the stability of everything settled on top of it. The upkeep of that foundation lies with each successive level above it until we finally arrive at the capstone. Rather than viewing themselves as modern-day Caesars, the leaders who embrace Responsibility more closely resemble caretakers. Being faithful to and providing for every aspect of their businesses—most especially the human aspect—leads to businesses being the best version of themselves. Loyalty and an assiduous work ethic are borne from this Responsibility. Ironically, this resembles a more principled version of the system we have striven to vanquish: Feudalism. The difference being that rather than a suppressive environment, it is more symbiotic in nature. By taking care of the people in his fiefdom, a lord's land prospers more. With the mindset of a caretaker, it is far more likely the lord will provide the resources to better ensure the viability and survivability of the fiefdom. On the other hand, if the lord manages his fiefdom in a tyrannical fashion which depletes his resources, nothing survives—including him. In the same sense, if the leaders in business manage in a way that values resources, the business has a far greater chance of being a going concern well into the future.

We have spoken of the Responsibility business leaders have towards their businesses in general and to their employees in particular. We should acknowledge that wage earners have no less a responsibility in their obligations to the workplace. Wage earners need to diligently perform the services for which they were hired and have enough sense to resist putting undue pressure on business leaders which may adversely motivate a business leader to reevaluate the operating parameters of the business. In other words: Don't incite a business leader to rethink location or employment for frivolous reasons.

Responsibility is the aether in which Power, Reputation, and Trust propagate. It plays a critical role in our interactions with other members of Society. The expertise by which we wield Responsibility can either attract or repulse people and opportunities. Its faithful and unceasing exercise ensures a maximizing of one's circumstances as they may be from time to time. Responsibility is not some superpower or some gift or some quality that is randomly distributed among humankind. We are all born with the same capacity to be

Responsible. Responsibility grows much like a muscle: The more you use it, the stronger it gets. And it all starts with one very simple step: Do what's Right.

On Voting

In our Society, we acknowledge that each and every citizen does not have enough time to actively participate in Government. The everyday person is far too busy pursuing happiness or, more probably, busying themselves with survival. Other priorities include work, raising a family, and engaging in social networking. This leaves little time for regular and frequent assemblies for the purpose of legislating or governing. We have adopted a representative system wherein we entrust certain individuals to take care of the business of Government. As in any other business, we expect the work to be done by qualified, experienced professionals. Just as no one would like their car repaired by a bee keeper, we also do not want the day-to-day running of our Government left to amateurs. Implicit in our expectation is that our representatives, firstly, duly prosecute the best interests of Society as a whole and, secondly, the best interests of their Constituency which best interests are conveyed to the respective representative through polling and direct interaction with their Constituency. This is a great

Responsibility and one that requires a person to forgo self-interest, personal sense of morality, and, in many cases, pride.

In his work, *The Leviathan*, Thomas Hobbes was quick to dismiss democracy as a suitable form of government because he observed that men were unable to put aside the influences of their personal convictions or of constituent pressure in order to do what was good for the society. But we are not Hobbesian, rather we are inheritors of the Great Experiment where the drafters of our Society believed in the ability of people to do exactly what Hobbes so eloquently asserts we cannot: To do what is Right. This means putting aside one's personal agenda for the good of our Society. While no one lives a life without entertaining some degree of darkness, our Social Contract demands that we believe that we are evolved enough, disciplined enough, dedicated enough to prove this founding principle true. It takes a unique motivation to want to serve in this faculty and an equally unique determination to pursue it as a career. It is a responsibility neither lightly taken nor lightly given. It is the expectation, duty, and responsibility of a representative.

The responsibility is no less great for the Constituency. They must determine who among them will be their representative. To ease this burden, our Society has provided a process by which a selection is made. This process has been a subject of numerous constitutional amendments wherein the subject of these amendments has been, for the most part, focused on easing the qualification of the voter and broadening the electorate to the extent that nearly every adult in the US is eligible to participate in an election.

Ideally, we want an informed and responsible voter going to the polls. We should encourage eligible voters to listen to the various arguments, research to separate fact from rhetoric, and come to a rational, emotionally detached decision as to the best candidate for representation. This analytical process can be time consuming; however, our obligations to the Social Contract require us to be diligent in this process. Otherwise how else can we be assured that the values upon which we set our Society continue in the future?

In a democracy—particularly in our Society—the right to vote should be based on being a part of a Constituency. A quick review of our Social Contract in the context of what lies between the Government and the governed delineates the reason to elect representatives. The basic premise, as the governed, is: We are conceding certain liberties to the Government in exchange for what they provide. Quite simply, we offer them funding and services. In return, the Government gives us safety, security, and infrastructure. That's it. Anything more is an infringement upon the individual rights of the people and will, ultimately, bias one faction over another, or obligate certain segments of people to provide to Government without a return on those provisions. By enabling Government to determine specific and special allocations of rights, money, or services without a supermajority of the Constituent is to transmogrify the Government into an institution that sets itself above the people and deems the people unable to decide for themselves what is Right and what is Wrong. The people are reduced to incompetents relying on an oligarchy to determine what is and what is not in their best interests. This is not our Society.

Since the Constituency has the responsibility to regulate Government, they first must have the capacity to understand Government and be aware of and familiar with the Social Contract they have *de facto* entered by virtue of being a member of the governed society. This occurs neither by heredity nor by osmosis. It is something that must be taught, questioned, and learned. In short, it requires a certain amount of effort on the part of the Constituency, particularly when it comes to being educated on the issues and diligently monitoring the actions taken by their representatives in relation to, first, the needs of the Society as a whole and, second, of their individual Constituencies.

The second requirement of the Constituency is that they must fulfill their obligations to the Government; *i.e.*, contribute their allotted portions of money and service. Only in meeting these obligations can they reasonably expect to receive the benefits that are conveyed by the Government. Such is the Social Contract. To be clear, any member of the Society who does not contribute both their fair portion of money and service is immediately disqualified from the Constituency. This must be so to avoid a skewing of representation, corruption of the Social Contract, and erosion of values. Without this criterion, a possibility exists whereby the non-contributing population can offset—or even outnumber—the contributing population. If these populations translate into voters, it is not only conceivable, but likely, that the duly elected representatives will feel obligated to the majority voters and not to the actual providers and enablers of Government. In fact, it would be their responsibility to weigh the will of the majority over the will of the minority even if the minority were to be the majority sponsors of the Government in terms of money and service. The consequence is a bias that disqualifies the Government as diligently fulfilling its contractual obligations as a government. A Constituency comprised of every member of society regardless of their contribution shifts the system from being a contractual one to a charitable one. Let us revisit one of the foundations of our Social Contract: Nothing is free.

We have on several occasions thus far mentioned the concept of service as a part of Society's obligations to Government, but we haven't, as yet, discussed what that could entail. It may be prudent to address that now. When someone mentions service with respect to Government, inevitably one of two things will immediately spring to mind: Civil service or military service. And with the latter comes flashbacks of involuntary conscription—the draft—that Government required on and off until 1973. Even today, our Society uses the Selective Service System that mandates every male in Society—legal and illegal—must register as a contingent to a potential future draft. But when we speak of service here, we are speaking of any contribution a member of Society can make to the Society through the Government out of their own abilities. That could be civil service or that could be military service, whichever best benefits the then present needs of Society. The reason service is important is quite simple: It makes us more nationalistic. Not as a zealot, but by dedicating part of one's life in contributing to Society, it makes a person invested in Society and, as a result, more engaged in its preservation. We care more about what the Government is doing at any point in time, and it makes us a bit better qualified to speak on it. Service unifies people, and any rivalries we see stem from pride in the accomplishments of which group did more to better Society knowing that all are contributors. How such a system would be structured is a discourse in itself, but dedicating three years—anything less doesn't seem like much of an investment—in some sector of Government would be a starting point.

If any person is not contributing their fair share to the Government out of that person's own resources, then that person is disqualified as a member of the Constituency. If a person is receiving more than what is defined by the Social Contract, that person is likewise disqualified. By example: An individual suddenly loses a job. The reason is unimportant. That person can no longer afford the necessities of living. Out of its Compassion, Society, through the dispensation of the Government, provides resources—whether financial or otherwise—to that individual for a period of time. As long as those provisions come from the contributions made by the Contributing Constituents to the Government, then the members of Society receiving these extraordinary benefits from the Government shall not be deemed as members of the Contributing Constituency for so long as they continue to receive such extraordinary benefits. In effect, they become wards of the state and, as such, shall be a disqualified member and shall not be permitted to vote or receive the same considerations as a Contributing Constituent. Just as in business when certain board members must recuse themselves in the event of a conflict of interest, so allowing the disqualified member a vote would have the potential to bias an election. If recipients of extraordinary benefits act in accordance with baser human nature, they would prefer to continue to receive an extraordinary benefit at the expense of the Contributing Constituents and at no expense to themselves.

This is not an argument to disallow extraordinary services. In an evolved society, there ought to be a mechanism whereby a person should be able to receive services that the Constituency, in their Compassion and through the proxy of their representatives, deems sufficient to provide. Rather it encourages a person to remedy their particular situation so as to re-enter the Constituency. Should they have no desire to become a Constituent, then they must, needs be, remain subject to the generosity of the Constituency as the Compassion of the Constituency changes and evolves from time to time.

With respect to elections and the exercise of the vote, we all too often hear: My vote doesn't count. This is the mantra of the ridiculous, and never was such an inane sentence ever uttered. Every vote counts. You can't reach ten without starting with one or without including six. But when the question is posed to a person on why they didn't vote, you are as likely to hear this answer as you are to inhale oxygen with your next breath. Unavoidably in the fallout of every election a certain number of people are disgruntled by the results, and, astonishingly, among them we find that a goodly portion of these voices come from those who didn't exercise their right to vote.

The disaffected—the losers of elections—point to the voting process and systems in place as reasons for failure or for non-participation. The allocations of districts in States or the use of the Electoral College in the Republic have, more than any fortress in time, been battered and assailed at the end of every election. It is difficult to find a balance that serves everyone. Certainly, any proponent of a popular vote must reside in the one of the few regions where Constituents are most concentrated. But the challenge is to, as best we can, weight electoral districts so that we do not isolate the people living in sparser populated areas; *e.g.*, the people who feed us. Our Society has solved that by establishing districts in States and the Electoral College in the Republic—both using population as a gauge. If we desire to improve upon those, we need systems that will not isolate our neighbors, will not ignore that our Republic is vast, will not ignore that our metropolitans are no more a contributor to our Society than our provincialities, and—most importantly—will provide a step forward in our evolution as a Society. In short, we must engage our Reason rather than our Emotion.

Perhaps no greater example of how indifference can affect an outcome lies with the 2016 presidential election. According to the Census Bureau, roughly 245.5 million Americans were of age to vote. Of that, only 157.6 million were registered to do so. That's 64%. So, 36% of our Society—about one in three—effectively abandoned their obligations under their Social Contract. One hundred and thirty-seven million voters participated in the 2016 election. That represents about 56% of all eligible voters. In a highly polarized bipartisan system such as ours, this translates into about 28% of total voters setting the course of Government. About one in four. Twenty-eight percent will be justified in their disappointment and the remainder should be silent; we should not countenance their opinion, particularly a negative one.

Voting participation in our Society is a right conferred to its Constituents; it is not a legal obligation *per se*. It is, however, an expectation under our Social Contract. For Government to provide us with safety, security, and infrastructure, it needs duly elected representatives. The selection of those representatives is made by its Contributing Constituents, whose obligation in this selection process it is to be familiar with candidates, to be intelligently informed with issues debated, and to determine who is best qualified to serve in Government, given the state and values of the Society at that time. It also calls upon us to sometimes make hard decisions. Real hard decisions. Sometimes we will be wrong. Other times we will get it right. But in times of where the tough call needs to be made, we should rise to the occasion rather than crumple under the weight of our citizenship.

At the present—and for quite some time now—registering to vote and casting that vote have been made so excruciatingly simple that few things are easier to do. It would be unconscionable to claim otherwise. Those of the Contributing Constituency who do not avail themselves of the electoral process ought to reflect on the qualities of the Society in which they live, the values of that Society, their contract with that Society, and their lifestyle in that Society. After such reflections, if their conscience prevents them still from becoming an active participant in voting or in exercising their duty as member of Society to be a part of its future, perhaps they should conclude that they would be far better in a different Society, one more suited to their passive values.

On Generations

If we were to track the evolution of a Society from its inception through all the generations leading up to the present, we would see a general trend whereby the present generation works to improve the circumstances for the next generation. A certain share of Society will think past that to the generations that come beyond the next but, by and large, the common Constituent will be more concerned about their immediate progeny. In short, they want to provide a better life for their children than they have; they want to give them the things that were unobtainable to them. As Society evolves and technology advances the quality and quantity of life, the things we look to give our children have become dilute in their importance. Where once a family wanted to provide electricity, running water, a basic—and eventually a higher—education, and a home, the focus has morphed into GI Joes with *kung fu* grip and Play Stations. Needs have given way to luxuries.

This is a double-edged sword for Society. It is Reasonable to expect that Society, as it matures, becomes better and more efficient at providing for the essential needs of the Constituency. It remains the main purpose of Society to resist stagnation and strive towards a more perfect version of itself. It is also the condition of humanity to exercise more Compassion as time and resources become more available. And so, it is only logical that needs, having been met through the contributions of generations of Society, make way for luxuries. In a sense it is a good thing: It shows that Society is a living organism growing to provide a better future for its Constituency while serving as a benchmark in Society's overall social and economic achievements.

The counter to this is when a generation attempts to better the life of its progeny through the satisfaction of their Emotion and this by catering to whimsical cravings. Society has been able, by virtue of its evolution and more efficient division of labor, to offer a great deal of options—perhaps too many—to keep its Constituents occupied in their free time. Moreover, as Society moves from an agrarian base to a manufacturing base to an information management base, the Constituency becomes less motile and gravitates toward a more sessile existence. As a consequence, what we consider to be enjoyable tends to occupy our minds rather than our bodies. With an overabundance of relatively inexpensive resources, it poses no difficulty at all to produce goods and services to placate the mind's imaginings, all the while destroying its physical host.

Were we to chart how much a generation has added to the next, we could imagine an avalanche in the quantity of goods and opportunities. And inevitably, the generation providing these to the next generation experiences an unconscious buyer's remorse. They become critical of the generation upon which these were bestowed and, acknowledging their offspring as inheritors of Society, despair. Descriptors like "lazy," "irresponsible," and "out of touch with reality" are tossed about in adult conversations, and somehow there arises a disconnect between the generations, neither one understanding the motivations or rationale of the other, all of which threatens a metaphorical break in the chain of a Society's evolution.

But here's the irony: A Society's values are either renewed or re-forged with the turning of each generation. In this, the condemning party is usually the guilty party. By not countenancing the values of the previous generation, we create a successive generation that we enable through our generosity and then, eventually and inexplicably, condemn them by the same generation's standards we ignored. This is the price of our generosity. While Right and Wrong are eternal, the culture and values that define a society need to be passed from one generation to the other. These aren't instinctive nor is there an innate awakening at a certain age in the development of our children. No hormone kicks in to reprogram a child. Teaching social mores to a child is akin to civilizing barbarians. To instill what is acceptable and unacceptable in society to a child takes patience, time, and resolve. Parenthood is not for the faint-hearted.

Experience is the best teacher. As long as it's someone else's experience; better they suffer the consequences, if any. Starting from infancy, children mimic what they see, particularly when they perceive the outcome as to their advantage. For good or bad, they become what is around them. They evolve into what they are exposed. These experiences are ingrained into their psyches, and they lean on them as what is normal in their world. Eventually, these values set the course they take in society and, if prevalent enough, become the ethos of the Society. The only tempering force is that of family. As the molecule is the smallest fundamental unit of a substance, so is the family the smallest fundamental unit of a society. The amalgamation of individual family values creates the values that define a society. Incongruous corruption of the family has the same effect to a society as rust in metal. It starts small, but quickly eats away at the host until parts of it are fragmented, weak, and easily broken. It is too easy to create a plethora of excuses to absolve ourselves from not doing our part in this respect. Most commonly, we blame our economic situation or our ethnic backgrounds. But these are excuses; human relationship is not regulated by money or color or race or religion or political affiliation. As of today, we have not found anything in our genome that would cause a person to act in such a fashion. Human relationships need to be nurtured at every stage of their development. In an attempt to absolve ourselves of any culpability, we desperately cling to the belief that whatever we do has an insignificant impact on our Society and amounts to little more than a rounding error in the big picture. But that cannot be true. As any chain is only as strong as its weakest link, so too, goes a society. In our acting as a strong link, we guarantee the strength of our Society. To do this we need not chase the horizon but simply think and act in each moment with Compassion.

When we step out to ten thousand feet and look down on our Society, it is easier to see how we have allowed our technology to overwrite itself on our need for interpersonal relations and—in many instances—replace it. Jean-Jacques Rousseau asserted that as technology of a society increases, so its moral quality decreases (Rousseau, 1750). In his 18th century world, that may have seemed a difficult concept to grasp and even more difficult to demonstrate. The world was not evolving at the break neck pace it has been in recent memory. But let us not personify technology so as to conveniently use it as a scapegoat for our short-sightedness. Technology is a tool and, as with many tools, its effectiveness is a consequence of the wielder. If a generation is chasing material gratifications, then technology is a means to that end. When those pursuits prove too much for the family unit, something needs to be sacrificed to achieve them. Generally, the next generation is all too gladly offered up to the gods of greed and avarice. And technology serves as the fire used to burn those sacrifices at the altar of gratification. To satiate the need for a quality of life—even if that quality of life is so obviously impractical or unachievable—we abandon our responsibilities to the Society and attempt to, individually, re-write the Social Contract to the extent that we no longer bear the onus to maintain the positive values that cost our predecessors so dearly. The result is unfortunate and long lasting. New terms enter our vocabulary that have no place in an evolved society; *e.g.*, latch key kids and the MTV generation.

At its root, a society is fueled by personal, human relationships. As communicative technology—through texts, email, and social media—usurp this basic building block, we find the fabric of our Society unraveling. Much, much too often impersonal communication has resulted in misunderstandings, confusion, animosity, and, ironically, *mis*communications. When we interact with one another, an involuntary bond develops—whether it be good or bad. Any businessman will tell you that it much more difficult to refuse someone in person than through written media. It is our nature to be social creatures, to want to be with other people, to want to interact with other people. When this happens, life happens. Problems are more readily solved. Compassion is more freely doled out. And we gravitate towards a single entity that we are calling our Society.

When we look at the next generation and criticize, or shrug our shoulders in confusion, or are dismayed at their habits, we are not condemning so much what they've become as what we've made them. It is like looking into the mirror at our failure. Rather than heaping disdain on them, we might better engage in self-flagellation in a meager attempt to atone to our ancestors who faithfully preserved the positive values we so shamelessly abandoned.

We are reaching a point in our evolution where we cannot give our children more than we had. Everything grows more accessible and affordable. This begs the question: What will those future generation give their children? Or will those generations be inconsolable?

On Immigration

Immigration in our Society is an important and key function in maintaining both the homogeneity of the Society—that is, to ensure that the values and ideals of Society as they exist from time to time are not diluted leaving the established members in the minority—and its heterogeneity, which is to import new ideas for Society to consider as it evolves. Society ought to value contributions that new members can make and, to that end, endeavor to facilitate the integration of outside individuals into Society. At the same time, Society must ensure that adequate entry criteria are in place to separate individuals that are able and willing to become Contributing members of Society from individuals that have neither the ability nor desire to contribute but who simply wish to subsist on the Compassion of Society. The Government, on behalf of the Constituency and through duly elected representatives, is responsible for creating these criteria, with such criteria necessarily being a reflection of the prevailing values of Society as they exist from time to time. The process to assess, and accept or reject new members should neither be overly bureaucratic nor unnecessarily exclusionary rather it should be, as much as possible given the innate complexities of evaluating peoples of different societies and cultures, straightforward and algorithmic in nature.

Such criteria are further designed so as not to disadvantage either the new member or the existing member of Society. Once an applicant is admitted to Society, it is the responsibility of the individual and the individual's family (if any) to immediately comply with the Social Contract and cultural norms as they exist at that time.

The primary overseer of immigration is the Government of the Republic. There are reasons for this. First, to assess the character of immigrants it will likely be necessary to interact with the society from which the immigrant is leaving. The representative of our Society to foreign nations is and has always been the Government of the Republic. This is consistent with our Social Contract whereby Government provides security and safety for the Constituents. Secondly, our Society is Republican in structure; that is, we are a coalition of, more or less, independent States in which trade and travel between member States is relatively uninhibited. Our Society has collectively agreed that any regulations required to provide for interstate activities should be a result of legislation by our duly elected representatives in the Government of the Republic. Since borders between states are open, it would be nonsensical that each State has their own criteria for immigration. Should one State be stricter than its neighboring state, an immigrant could simply enter into the State with the laxer criteria and then cross the border into the stricter State. There would no way to monitor that kind of diaspora in our Society.

Foremost in any immigration process is the ability of the immigrant to be a Contributing member of the Society. It neither serves Society as a whole or the existing members individually to assume burdens other than those that, at any given time, apply to the prevailing state of Society. The primary concern of any society is its survival. We ought not sacrifice our values, our own futures, or those of generations to come because we are empathetic to peoples outside our Society. It is unfortunate that there will likely always be those outside our Society who suffer or whose quality of life is a mere shadow of ours. It is an equally unfortunate fact that we cannot help them all. We simply do not have the resources.

Illegal immigration has been a topic that seems to always end in heated debates among different sectors in our Society. This makes one wonder why. As perhaps the best example of the most succinct summary of the issue, Sonny Bono was once asked what his position was on illegal immigration. He simply replied, “It’s illegal.” Really there’s nothing more to be said. If we find ourselves taking the opposite side of something that has been legislated by our duly elected representatives, then it might either be time for new legislation or for us to re-evaluate our position. It should not make criminals out of us. It is our Responsibility to conform with the Laws set by our Government. Illegalities cannot be tolerated if for no other reason than it is Wrong. Our whole Society is predicated upon the individual knowing what is Right and doing it. When we succumb to Emotion, then we find ourselves doing what is Wrong but convincing ourselves it's Right. In the blink of an eye, we suddenly want to transmogrify from a democrat to a Hobbesian: We decide to take back the rights we ceded because we feel our Government is no longer suitable to our immediate individual pursuits or, more precisely, our personal and corrupted sense of what Right is at the time. But we are not Hobbesians, we are, in fact, democrats. It is not a value of our Society to whimsically abandon certain discrete fair standards just to get what we want. The expectation of our Society is that, while we can feel Emotion, we have the discipline to act with Compassion.

A twin motivator to Emotion in supporting the illegal immigrant is usury. There are among us those that would take advantage of the illegal immigrant's plight for their own gain. For obvious reasons, an illegal alien wants to stay as far below the radar as possible. This allows for no small degree of blackmail by those who are aware of their situation and who would indenture them under conditions far below those which our Society finds acceptable. The illegal consents to this only because these conditions may still be much better than the ones in their previous life and that they have no desire to be identified and deported. This is a failing of our values in those who abandon integrity in favor of personal gain.

When caught, these usurers claim that the illegals are filling positions that no one in the Constituency wants or would do, and so many turn a blind eye. Jobs and salaries are economical in nature and make a weak excuse for criminality. Labor has always been reflected in end costs and impacts businesses in one of two ways: Greater profits or cheaper goods. The core of this issue is not so much the producer of goods or the provider of services than our individual desire to attain as many goods and services as we can with the limited financial resources we have. In short, we do not want to do without. Particularly, after we have had a taste for those things. To enforce immigration standards is to, in some ways, cause each of us to re-assess what goods and services we can afford. And while to support these standards is expected under our Social Contract—as they were set through the legislation of our duly elected representatives—it will have an impact on our daily lives. For some that will be bigger than others, but the impact will trickle down to us all in some form. Nevertheless, profitability is no excuse for criminality.

Too often the face of the illegal immigrant comes in two flavors: The child and the criminal. Our Society has drifted, unfortunately, to polar extremes when it comes to this issue. We see the face of a child of an illegal and are flooded with Emotion so strong it's enough to compel us to attempt to void Laws to which we agreed. It is a tragic thing when a parent is separated from a child when the former is illegal and the latter, born in our Society, is not. The choice was not the child's, but neither was it Society's. It was the parent's. The reason why the parent chose to have the child after crossing the border is irrelevant. Under our Laws, the child is a legal member of our Society; the parent is not. Emotion plays no part here. We may invoke Compassion and, judicially, make allowances for this circumstance; however, when exceptions to standards outnumber the rule, there is a problem with the standards.

Crime comes with immigration, even with legal immigration. Our Society is a particularly well situated one when it comes to quality of life, financial opportunities, and abundance of material goods. The lazy and weak minded will always walk among us. Unfortunately, when you add strength of body or of numbers to that, a segment of Society is born that takes what they want from the weaker or the outnumbered. Hurdles in language, undue discrimination in the workplace, and preconceptions of race or religion are a few contributing factors that might serve as an impetus for any individual immigrant to become discouraged and turn to the dark side. Those reasons are more a failing of the Society than the individual. On the other hand, there are wicked, evil people—general those weak in mind and spirit—that prefer to do Wrong than Right. Some enjoy it. For them, it is easier to take than make. These people have no place in our Society. Once identified, incarceration and/or deportation must proceed as quickly as our Laws allow.

In our Society, we, as the Constituency, are provided certain rights and processes that protect us from wrongful prosecution and guarantee a due process of our Laws. We have allowed for these rights and processes to extend to legitimate guests in our Society. We are not obligated to extend them to the uninvited or illegal. Under these circumstances, how we adjudicate illegal immigrants will depend on the prevailing policies of the time and to what extent we desire to be Compassionate.

For illegals not involved in perpetrating crime, hard choices need to be made; there are no fairy tale endings. An illegal parent must be deported otherwise we illegitimately negate our Laws. A legal child can opt to stay or can opt to leave with the parent. Should the child leave, that child can, at any time, return. Under our Laws the child legally is member of our Society. The parent may also return after completing the immigration process. A judiciary may, through acts of Compassion, make certain allowances for the parent to reside, legally, in our Society. These acts must be sparse in number so as not to effectually void the Laws set by duly elected legislators and not to put an unreasonable onus on Society. There needs to be some particular and uniquely compelling reasons for Compassion. Again, Society is faced with these burdens through no fault of its own; it had no input into the choices made which have landed parent and child in these situations. No matter how we feel, we cannot shrink away from or be repulsed by the enforcement of the Laws that have been emplaced through legislation and by our duly elected representatives. Enforcement is the Right thing to do and is expected under our Social Contract. Should we find ourselves in the position where the enforcement becomes unconscionable, it is time for different legislation. Our Society provides a path for that.

Immigration is an important part of a Society's growth and evolution. Regrettably, it is all too often bogged down with polarizing disagreements within the Constituency as to how this is best served. Argument and discussion are healthy parts of establishing processes when we are all tacking towards the same port. When we begin to tolerate or make excuses for illegalities, we can safely say that either the process is broken or that those of the Constituency who are promoting disobedience to duly established standards have lost their way and are not acting responsibly within the context of our Social Contract. The former is easy to fix through legislation; the latter not so much so. To rein in Emotion or greed oftentimes requires firm and unpleasant measures. We would all like to believe that positive reinforcement is the solution. This, however, is a long and arduous path; time consuming to the point of the impractical. To drink from the cup of negative reinforcement is repulsive, but it does give nearly immediate corrective action. And should a member of our Society prefer to ignore the basic premise of our Social Contract—that is, to do what is right—it leaves the enforcers and adjudicators of our Laws little other choices.

On the Fourth Estate

Ted Turner is responsible for the polarization of America.

More than any man on Earth, he has masterminded (likely by accident) the erosion of societal cooperation, unity, and bipartisan dialogue, all the while promoting anarchy with a blatant disregard for all the progress our Society has made over the 200 hundred years it has striven to mature and become a more harmonious and tolerant people. His vehicle for the destruction of Society? CNN.

The birth of CNN News in 1980 was a novel leap for television at the time. It provided national news in 30-minute loops, being updated as new stories broke. As with any novelty, there was an initial surge in viewership and then a rationalization of those numbers. Busy people enjoyed the freedom of being able to catch up with the country and the world at any time during the day or night and were glad not to be committed to an hour between six and seven for the evening news, or eleven to eleven-thirty for the day's wrap up. Traveling businessmen, in particular, tuned in, not so much to watch but to listen as they prepared themselves for the day or to wind down as the day ended. This particular demographic ensured the early success of the station; hotels scrambled to subscribe to the independent network.

But things changed in 1981. Walter Cronkite, dubbed at one point the "most trusted man in America," retired. For two decades, his reporting was the stalwart voice of the media. No nonsense, and delivered in an even, matter-of-fact tone, he would always end the broadcast with his signature: "And that's the way it is, January 22nd 1973" (or any other date). Credible and believable, he left the interpretation of events to the viewer, and his absence left a void in the media. The networks raced to provide the next most trusted man. He never arrived.

Although it's been 40 years since Mr. Cronkite left the scene, networks are still vying to be the be-all and end-all, go-to source for information. One way to gain support in any competitive endeavor is to get someone invested in your cause. Emotionally invested. A logic-based argument is a lengthy one, and it persists until all the available data is laid out, analyzed, and conclusions reached. Then it is over. It is an exhausting but comprehensive process and, in a purely logical exercise, both sides of the issue eventually arrive at the same conclusion. Unfortunately, social issues are not so binary, especially if the fates of people are involved. It is in our base nature to have some feelings towards these kinds of issues and they typically invoke some Emotional response. This response, consciously or unconsciously, dictates our initial position on the issue. To temper this strong Emotional bias, we rely on thousands of years of critical thinking to direct our efforts to arrive at a Compassionate, sagacious outcome. But what we have seen in recent times is, instead, a reversion to our Neanderthal origins whereby we assert our strong, unbridled Emotions, and whoever does not share in that emotion is labeled as zealot, radical, inane, unsympathetic, and un-American. A new enemy is born.

How did this setback in our evolution occur? Talk radio. Talk television. Discussing issues beyond the confines of their relevance in Society or drawing out issues far past their expiration date. We speak *ad nauseam* about the same things with no new perspectives over and over again; there is no progress, just more and more Emotion miring us down preventing solutions. Watching any debate on an issue is like watching an American trying to communicate in a foreign country: To better make the other side understand, they repeat the same thing over and over again, and each time more loudly and more slowly. Happily, for conspiracy theorists, the media has provided an ample venue for these heated exchanges. Sadly, we only need to look to our five- and six-year old children arguing over a swing on the playground for the same effect.

Thirty-minute news loops waned in popularity, and so the media moguls needed a new schtick to influence their audiences if they were going to assume the mantle of Mr. Cronkite. This prompted them to contrive a new fashion that would both advance their own agendas and increase their profits. Anchor people became more animated, sometimes shouting at the viewers like some Crazy Eddie commercial. Concurrent interviews with split screens between opposing factions became more and more commonplace. Individual agendas came to the fore thinly veiled as news. The media was invoking Emotional responses in its viewership. New stations popped up to accommodate the disaffected until today we see such specific and polarized Emotional overtures in our news that it is nearly impossible for the average Constituent to discern what is opinion and what is fact. The tragedy in this is that we have, traditionally, relied on the media to keep us intelligently informed of our country and our world that so we might better navigate life and better know how to maintain our Society and its values. To find these sources today is not something we can do with any degree of confidence.

The media has been traditionally referred to as the Fourth Estate. The origins of this date back to the early 19th century. Until that time, the British Parliament had traditionally consisted of three estates: The Lords Spiritual, the Lords Temporal, and the Commons, or, more simply, the church, the nobility, and the commoners. The term "fourth estate" stems initially from the 1837 publication *The French Revolution: A History* by Thomas Carlyle and more specifically in his 1841 publication *On Heroes and Hero Worship.* In the latter, Carlyle cited Edmund Burke's comment in 1787 when Parliament was debating the merit of opening up press reporting in the House of Commons. According to Carlyle, Burke remarked that there were, "Three Estates in Parliament, but, in the Reporters' Gallery yonder, sat a Fourth Estate more important far than they all."

Burke, and subsequently Carlyle, were pointing out that the media holds sway over the minds and opinions of the common people. By controlling what gets printed and in what fashion, they have a great power to influence Society on a number of broad and far-reaching issues. Historically, Constituents tend to believe, naively, the media to be unbiased and expert at fleshing out details that the Government wishes to suppress. The reliance—or overreliance—on the press grows out of mistrust of the Government and the duly elected representatives. This comes to pass because men who are in positions of Responsibility do what is Wrong and not what is Right. Conspiracies, corruption, nepotism, and an overall lack of transparency have, over time, served to throw up walls of skepticism and clouds of suspicion herding the Society in the arms of a body that seems to have their best interest at heart. And this usually done by confirming our skepticisms and suspicions.

What we have lost sight of is that the media picks and chooses what they want to report. They determine what issues are relevant and which are not. Acknowledging that not every bit of news can be reported—limits on time and space make this impractical—it is an interesting observation to note that different news agencies tend to report the same stories. This seems to be true whether it be of national or local news, and it appears to be more consistent in electronic media than in print. While there are, certainly, criteria that drives what makes news and what does not, the Fourth Estate has evolved into an efficient social filter that all too subtly drives the values and the direction of Society. By introducing divisiveness into its play book, more of Society relies on the media rather than themselves to forge opinions and thought. This leads to a barely controlled anarchy where we are driven not by what Government does but how that is interpreted by the media. The liberties taken by the media today make the yellow journalism of William Randolph Hearst seem milquetoast in comparison.

Our Fourth Estate has morphed from an information source to a societal puppeteer, and our tacit approval can only mean that we would prefer to be Hobbesian and not democratic; that is, we prefer to have someone tell us what to think and what to believe. Have we lost the will to make our own decisions when presented with facts? Are we so concerned with being on Team Democrat or Team Republican that we forget why there are either? Have we so lost sight of our Social Contract to the point that we would preferred to be dictated to rather than to be of our own minds? Each Constituent needs to be of their own conviction; to posit that our Society would willingly forfeit the right to think as they please would be a tremendous suspension-of-disbelief.

Being so far down this rabbit hole, how do we restore our confidence in the Fourth Estate? Oddly enough, by ignoring them. This seems counterintuitive since we rely on our media to keep us informed with the goings on in the country and the world. Until our Society's media can redeem themselves, it would seem a better choice to source information from outside that pool. From a source that is not Emotionally vested in the outcomes of the issues or the sensitivities of the stories. Reuters. BBC. Le Monde. Japan Times. Al Jazeera. Der Speigel. A shift to these news sources by our Society will, slowly and undoubtedly, signal to our media that we have had enough of their hype and are looking for news not nonsense. As more and more Constituents turn to these more reliable and less sensational news sources, advertising dollars will follow. Advertising profits will allow these sources to grow and displace the Emotion-mongers that, today, plague our airwaves and our presses, and who assault our minds with a goal to divide and destroy a long-standing Society. Society needs to be informed, not influenced.

On Guns

We have a unique Society in that we have been baptized in the holy water of firearms. While our ancestors in the Old World were born from the age of lances, bows, swords, and pikes, we forged our land with blackened fingers and singed cheeks all the while reeking of sulfur and saltpeter. The pull of a trigger and flash from the muzzle gave us dominion over the New World. In the earliest parts of our Society, the gun was as likely to be found in any home as a hammer. And like the hammer, it was a necessary tool: It provided protection and sustenance.

As our Society grew, the reliance on firearms grew. It often proved the deciding factor between life and death. And so a great part of our ingenuity was focused on making a better and more efficient firearm. The Lancaster rifle, the Hawken percussion rifle, the lever action Winchester and Henry rifles, Samuel Colt's Peacemaker, the Gatling gun, the Garand, the eternal 1911A1, the M14, M16, and M5 assault rifles, all striving for a more perfect weapon. The access to these tools has been typically limited only by what quality one could afford. The need for them was undoubtable.

But as our Society evolved, one would have hoped that the need for such tools would become obsolete. We see this in our European and Asian cousins. Yet, we still obsess ourselves with the owning and the use of these antiquated and largely unnecessary tools. Since our founders provided for the right of firearm ownership in the Constitution, it is not an issue so easily dismissed nor one so easily resolved to the satisfaction of all Constituents. The original rationale for the second amendment has been lost in speculation, in interpretation, and, mostly, in the passage of time. In those days, a standing militia was still needed; the Government had not yet enough resources to form an adequate standing Army nor were the municipalities of time—disadvantaged by poor infrastructure, slow modes of transport, and too few people occupying too large a land—able to provide a law enforcement body to effectively police its confines. A family's protection against the hostiles of the wilderness—whether it was man or beast—depended on their possession and skill with a weapon. A gun.

The domestication of the physical expanse into what we now consider the entirety of the Republic occurred over the span of decades, so the need to keep a firearm culture *in situ* was never in question. In part, it defined who we were as a Society. And even today looking from outside our Society, it still distinguishes us from the rest of the world. The first image conjured of Americans in other countries is that of the cowboy and the six-shooter. As urbanization overwrote frontier life, the absolute need for every family to own a firearm waned until it has now virtually disappeared. Better manned law enforcement agencies sprouted and grew into organizations that were able to cover larger and larger areas, both in the States and in the Republic. Despite this growth, however, the vastness of our land possessions still sees a number of our Constituents living in remote and isolate places where 911 is just to let the authorities know where to find the bodies. It can be, thusly, argued by the Constituents inhabiting those areas that as long as there are elements of our Society that are determined to do Wrong and advance themselves through violence, there will always be a need for the private ownership of firearms.

The vigor demonstrated by many Constituents to retain the ability to purchase and own firearms of every sort is only matched by that of many other Constituents who believe that our Society should evolve into a gun free society. The debate, far from empirical, has gained fervor and momentum especially in the light of mass shootings. It has become one where our Society can no longer disregard the stagnation of progress which denies us a solution that will save lives—many of which are our children's. Neither can we be mired down in complicated processes that required a myriad of legislative acts not the least of which may be the repealing of a constitutional amendment in the Bill of Rights; a core list of rights added to the Constitution partially to elucidate the fundamental grants of the Government to its citizenry without which it would've been unlikely that the Constitution we know would've been ratified (Ellis, 2015).

Theoretically and if each citizen would be responsible in firearm ownership, there would be no national discussion on the subject. There would be no mass shootings and no firearms used in the conduct of crimes. Unfortunately, this is not the circumstance in which we find ourselves. Lax firearm ownership, irresponsible firearm use, citizens who are incapable of basic problem solving and who vent their Emotions through the use of firearms on their fellow citizen, and a general disregard for firearm safety have escalated the topic of firearms to a bitter and fractious debate. When the Constituents of a society cannot, of themselves, do what is Right and best for Society, it sets the regrettably stage wherein the Government must determine what is best. This is a terrible blow for our Society; a loss for the democrat and a win for the Hobbesian.

When cooking a frog, if you throw it into a pot of boiling water, it will jump out. If you put it, instead, in cold water and slowly heat it, the frog will sit there and happily cook. In this fashion, a drastic change was made over time and was acceptable to the affected organism. The same stratagem ought be applied to Society's gun issue. The acts that will be required to garner the immediate results we desire seem too drastic to a large enough sector of our Constituents that they will likely never come to pass. The confiscation or registering of all firearms is a daunting task and one that is truly impractical. Aside from search and seizure—illegal in itself—Society will never be sure that all firearms are accounted for and that no unregistered firearm will be used in a crime. And in the end, there is a constitutional right to own. They say stupidity is the repetition of doing the same thing over and over again and expecting different results. We have been trying to reign in our firearm culture for years by doing the same things over and over, but haven't made any progress. Let's not reinforce failure; it's time to find a different path forward.

Guns don't kill people; people kill people. We hear this all the time from gun advocates. They are right in the sense that a firearm is a just a hunk of plastic and metal, inert and without a conscience. The wielder determines how and when it is used. But let's make no mistake: A firearm's primary function is to kill. A long barrel at long range; a pistol at close range. A long barrel firearm has more versatility in that it can be used for hunting and so can be an asset to one's existence. A pistol, on the other hand, has been designed since its inception to kill another human. Very, very few people are proficient enough to hunt with a handgun. Too many people have the image of John Wayne riding his horse and shooting the black hat off the saloon rooftop. Most handguns are good to about 25 feet. Beyond that range requires talent or a great deal of practice, but at the very least a skill that does not, naturally, run through the DNA of the common man. How do we balance the inert object with the emotional fragileness of the human psyche? By focusing on what really does kill people.

Guns don't kill people; bullets do. Herein lies the irony. We spend so much time trying to limit firearms that we overlook the fact that they are useless without ammunition. One can buy firearms to one's heart desire, but without ammunition, all one would have would be wall ornaments. Were Society to focus on limiting ammunition sales, it may prove easier than legislating around an impossible amendment to the Bill of Rights. So, as the first step in turning the heat up to cook the frog, we should consider limiting purchases of ammunition, including re-loading materials.

Zeroing a weapon optimally takes nine rounds of ammunition. Confirmation of the zero another three. That's twelve rounds. In hunting, a reasonably competent marksman will use no more than three rounds per target; a proficient one requires only a single shot. To entertain more than the former should raise a flag to the prospective hunter as to their adequacy and ability to hunt. In times of the rifled flintlock—a weapon that takes the best marksman a minute and a half to re-load—hunters could amply feed their families. Do we find ourselves so diminished hundreds of years later that we rely on a spate of gunfire to neutralize one target? Hardly not. With advances in gunsmithing and manufacturing, even our single shot firearms require less skill than those of the past. So, it stands to reason, then, that at any given time possession of twenty rounds of ammunition for a particular caliber should be a sufficient supply of ammunition. Therefore, limiting the sales of ammunition in a particular caliber to forty rounds for a single firearm owner would appear to be more than reasonable. To plug the hole of stockpiling ammunition through multiple purchases made at different sales points, the purchaser would need to return a certain portion—let's say 75%—of the spent brass (the brass being specially marked to distinguish it from ammunition purchases outside this system) of that caliber from previous purchases prior to being sold new cartridges.

Now it is unreasonable to expect a new firearm owner to become proficient after firing only forty rounds. It takes a hundred rounds to break in a firearm and hundreds more to become adept at using it. And even then, zeroing with nine rounds for some just isn't possible. This is where the creation of federally regulated gun ranges becomes an interesting prospect. These facilities would provide an assortment of basic services: an armory where a firearm owner would be able to store firearms; sale of ammunition in unlimited quantities where such ammunition must be used at the facility; firearm/marksman instruction; and various target lanes to accommodate all skill levels, and all in a secure and safe environment. It would allow for a firearm owner to shoot as many rounds as they like without the burden of having to collect and return brass and make several trips back and forth to a dealer. Ammunition is purchased without limitation provided that it all be expended there. Consequently, firearm owners could practice marksmanship to any degree they saw fit in order to become more proficient and, at the same time, conduct that activity in a safe, secure location. As the onus for safety and security under our Social Contract falls upon the Government, it would stand to reason that these ranges would fall under the purview of the Government for regulation and licensing.

The image that comes to mind is a cold, loud sterile facility. Concrete and stalls. Not necessarily so. With forethought, some of these ranges could, conceivably, evolved into public/private clubs where, after some shooting, one could relax over a dinner and a couple drinks. We see this perfected in shooting clubs with our British cousins. And this concept is not so different in how we go about doing our other recreational activities. We go to ski mountains to ski; we go to bowling alleys to bowl, we go to lakes to boat, we go to camp sites to camp, we go to golf courses to golf. Like shooting, these activities are not something the majority of Society can do in their backyards, yet we happily travel to locations where we can enjoy them. In time, the same mindset will confer on the shooting sportsman.

This scheme does not affect ammunition already stockpiled by private firearm owners. Those stockpiles, however, will approach zero in time. The general rule is that ammunition is good for ten years. In theory, however, if ammunition is kept away from extreme heat and cold and is stored in a dry place, it should last indefinitely. Still, it would take a brave soul to fire a round that is 30 years old. So, the firearm owner has a couple options on stockpiled ammunition: Rotate it out with new ammunition purchases maintaining a net-sum-zero inventory; or shoot rounds in excess of what is permitted through sales thereby reducing their inventory. In the former case, Society is no worse off than it is now in that the quantity of ammunition in firearm owner hands has been capped. In fact, firearm owners may be even more reluctant to use those caches in the knowledge that they cannot be replenished. In the latter case, there will be little impact in the short-term, but as firearm owners use ammunition faster than they can resupply, Society will realize an overall reduction in privately held ammunition. In either scenario and even without restricting firearms sales, the use of firearms outside authorized shooting ranges will invariably decrease.

The second step in cooking our frog is to determine what types of firearms make sense to be kept in a private residence. This is not to say this determines or limits or constitutes the entire complement of firearms a citizen could own, but only those that can be kept in that Constituent's residence. Those firearms that are not permitted in a private residence may still be purchased, but they would need to be stored in an armory and used exclusively at an authorized shooting range. In this fashion no second amendment rights have been violated.

Essentially, we own firearms for three reasons: protection, hunting, and recreation. We need to be reasonable in our choice of what type of firearms we use in each instance, which reasonableness is a reflection of our environment, relative risks, and technology. The main goal is to make the marksman—not the firearm—the key component. Firearms are not idiot proof; one needs a certain knowledge and no small amount of skill to be safe and proficient. The better armed with these qualities, the less a marksman needs in a firearm—for any purpose. Conversely, the more inept the marksman, the more is needed in a firearm to compensate for that incompetence. A true marksman always rises to the level of the firearm, not *vice versa*. We need to keep this in the fore as we deliberate on the types of firearms Society allows in private residences. In other words: We should hold firearm owners to a high standard of firearm handling practices and proficiency and demand they be responsible in the perfection and maintenance of this craft. With this as the premise, we can then better determine what kind of firearm makes sense in a private residence for use in various applications.

Looking at the operation—or the mechanical action—of firearms, we can relegate firearms into one of four categories: automatic (continuously fires rounds as long as the trigger is pressed), semiautomatic (able to fire repeatedly through an automatic reloading process but requiring release and another pressure of the trigger for each successive shot), repeating (firearm capable of several repeated shots following a manual single ammunition reload stored in a magazine), and single shot (firearm must be manually reloaded after each shot). To choose which is best in a situation depends on the collection of circumstances in that situation, not the least of which is the desired outcome. But we needn't use an anvil to kill an ant when a newspaper will do; we should settle on the lowest denominator.

Since we are not in the zombie apocalypse and no scenario comes to mind wherein a private Constituent would need to have a firearm that has a 600 round cyclic rate of fire, it would be reasonable to conclude that there is no need for a private Constituent to possess an automatic weapon in the home. In the pursuit of recreation, an automatic weapon has no peer. It is, even for the most reticent of enthusiasts, exceedingly enjoyable to fire and is not beyond providing an addictive and infectious thrill. Yet, that is born of a purely Emotional response, devoid of any practicality. Again, absent a force-on-force armed conflict, when would we need that kind of firepower? The military has since stopped issuing shoulder arms weapons with fully automatic capabilities. Moreover, even if the Founding Fathers thought that we should retain gun ownership to provide for the revolution and overthrow of the any at the time existing Government, we can no longer expect that in this day of advanced military weaponry a small caliber automatic weapon could prevail against the armament held by our military. We would have less than a wisp of a chance of defeating a well-organized, well-funded, and better equipped standing army. We can give a nod for automatic firearms as recreation, but certainly not as something that is pertinent to the survivability of our Society. And, not for nothing, the potential of these firearms in irresponsible hands invites tragic consequences and in such numbers that should only be found on a battlefield.

With regard to semiautomatic firearms, they exist for two reasons: to engage a large number of targets in a short period of time; and to compensate for poor marksmanship. To date, there has been no recorded mass attack by deer or bear or skunks on a private residence. Furthermore, to employ a semiautomatic firearm to mask incompetence should be a point of shame and embarrassment to any marksman. With respect to our premise of firearm ownership—that is, to have the firearm owner invested in the learning, proficiency, and mastery of the firearm—it follows that this category of firearm also is not something we would expect to find in a private Constituent's home. For protection, an incompetent marksman can only hope to get themselves and/or their families killed. A competent marksman needn't fire more than a few shots to discourage intruders or assailants; particularly, in this day and age wherein law enforcement agents are soon to respond and wherein handheld video or modern surveillance systems can readily capture the identities of the assailants.

Repeating firearms are limited in the size of their magazines and in the amount of time they require to cycle from one round to another. These seem appropriate for novice and intermediate marksmen as they provide multiple—but very limited—shots on targets. With respect to protection, a repeating arm still provides several shots on target before closure. A key deterrent in any assault scenario is shock and awe. That can be done with an automatic firearm, but we should keep in mind that only the first round lands where it is aimed; the rest are randomly spattered about. This invites untended and collateral damage…perhaps to one's own home. On the other hand, nothing can be more nerve shattering than the sound of a large bore shotgun blast at close range. Met with this welcome, few would continue an invasion of a home knowing that, within minutes, law enforcement agents would be responding and then they would be assailed on two fronts. Absent a well-coordinated, premeditated attack launched against a private homestead and on a unprecedent scale, there seems, in the realm of protection, no rationale in having more than a repeating firearm to stave off such an attack; particularly, if the marksman is proficient in shooting. In the pursuit of game, an adequate knowledge of ballistics and marksmanship can serve as surety to provide meat on the table. A surer way is your local Safeway. The conclusion here is that we should see no objection to finding a repeating firearm in a private residence provided it is stored in a secure location within that residence.

Dieu ne pas pour le gros battalions, mais pour sequi teront le meilleur (Voltaire, 1735).

God is not on the side of the big battalions, but the best shots.

Single shot firearms serve as the pinnacle of firearm mastery and to a level of marksmanship that all aspire. One shot; one kill. Only expert marksmen can boast this honor since the firearm can only deliver one shot at a time and reloading often takes too long to provide a second shot on a moving target. We've manufactured these since before the Revolutionary War, and only the best-of-the-best can have and maintain proficiency with these weapons. Indeed, this is the Holy Grail of standards. Single shot firearms are generally more difficult to master, but once done, they can be used for any purpose. Given the scope and depth of their limitations, it is doubtful that there would be any reasonable objection to having these in a private residence.

One clarification that is an important footnote in this paradigm: Automatic and semiautomatic firearms may still be purchased, just not kept at a private residence. These firearms would be stored at a Government sanctioned gun range, and there in a secure armory. The Constituent would be able to use that firearm only at that (or another authorized) range. In this fashion, these types of firearms would be removed from the general public but still provide their owners with recreation, a recreation that would otherwise soon disappear once existing, privately held ammunition had been expended and the limitations on new ammunition purchases enacted.

The security of firearms held by a Constituent in a private residence is the individual Constituent's sole responsibility. With exception of a reported theft, the consequence of any incident resulting from the use or misuse of a firearm owned by a Constituent—accident or no—is borne by that Constituent. Those consequences may also be conferred upon other individuals, but the Constituent is not exempt merely because the incidence was perpetrated by another. Owning firearms requires a certain degree of sense. Lest we forget, the purpose of any firearm is to kill.

We will never be able to account for or reign in the number of firearms and the countless rounds of ammunition already in Society. We shouldn't set this as an expectation and should give up any notion that this will ever become a reality. We can, however, limit in the future how much more we add to these untold numbers of privately held firearms, and we can control how and to what extent they can be used. Automatic and semiautomatic firearms use up vast quantities of ammunition with each use, and those numbers can't be replenished if there are limits on ammunition sales to Constituents. Soon, those firearms, if still in a private residence, won't be practical to fire: Forty rounds would be spent in about 26 seconds. By offering storage and use of Government ranges, we increase the security and accountability of those firearms while still providing the owners the means to enjoy them as firearm connoisseurs. Furthermore, we increase the safety of the general public *vis-à-vis* reducing the ability to use firearms in mass shootings or active shooter scenarios. After just a few years, the frog will be cooked, and we will have evolved into a Society that will have maintained an environment for firearm enthusiasts, but will have removed the harbinger of wanton public tragedies.

On Healthcare

Healthcare, as an issue, is radioactive; no one really wants to touch it. We continually hear about it in Government because it's such a touchstone issue, but any solution is bound to be met with waves-crashing-on-the-beach criticism. Mainly because there's too little thought given in the charge to get a too quick remedy legislated. But despite being controversial, despite the public uproar, and despite all the eyes looking to Government for a solution, there is no obligation under our Social Contract for Government to address this issue. They need only to ensure pharmaceuticals, medical devices, and associated facilities are safe; to ensure that healthcare providers are qualified and do not endanger Constituents; and to maintain infrastructures that support state-of-the-art medicine and medical systems. Individuals are at liberty to choose their own level of medical care; a decision they must weigh in determining the kind of lifestyle they wish to live.

We all complain about how much we pay for healthcare. We think that the nebulous "they" are over charging us and becoming disproportionally wealthy at our expense. The plain fact is: Healthcare is inherently expensive. And in this instance, it truly is a case where you get what you pay for. This is not to say that healthcare costs can't be significantly reduced. They can. But what we need to understand is that even were that to happen, it is still going to be expensive. We need to be at peace with that. To help achieve that peace, it may be useful to illustrate why it cost so much in the first place.

If we look at the pharmaceutical segment of the healthcare industry, we find a case study in failure. Less than one out of twenty compounds being tested as therapies survive the development and regulatory process and make it to market. If we account for those failures, the out-of-pocket cost for an approved drug runs about $2 billion, and when capitalized much more (DiMasi, 2018). Now imagine the financial needs of a company that is trying to develop 30 drugs across four therapeutic areas. To feed that R&D monster, companies need a huge war chest rife with cash. That cash comes from the revenue streams of the drugs that do survive the grueling regulatory process and make it to market.

Unfortunately, we can't amortize those costs over a long period of time and over the entire stable of drugs a company may market. If we could, the equation would be simple: Cost = Manufacturing cost + 20%. The problem is drug exclusivity has a relatively short life span before faced with generic competition. After a drug completes five to eight years of grueling and expensive studies, at least a year-and-a-half regulatory review process, and finally an approval by the Food and Drug Administration (FDA), Government provides a four-year regulatory exclusivity period. This exclusivity only prevents a third party from using or referencing the data the originator company has filed with the FDA (generic manufacturers reference this data and so need not expend resources—particularly money—in clinical trials allowing them to go straight to market making the drug more affordable). That period can be longer if the originator has patent protection on the drug or on its therapeutic indication. Depending on the extensiveness of and time required for the development program, a drug can fend off generic competition for a time of between five to ten years. This is the window a company has to generate $2 billion on that drug.

A complication to this is that America—through its free pricing system—funds drug development for the entire world. While that seems a bold statement, it rings true. Most countries have agencies that regulate how much a company can charge for their drugs. When those market prices are compared to the same drug as marketed in America, we often see a large disparity. Without sales in America, many of these companies couldn't continue to fund their research or drug development programs. This price difference unsettles us, and we feel that drug companies are taking advantage of our free pricing system. And to some extent they are. But let's remember, that's a double-edged sword. We criticize the scientific community for not developing cures for certain diseases or for focusing on one therapeutic area more than another. But if we ask them to reduce drug prices, that situation only grows direr. Companies will need to make hard choices on what to market, and these decisions will more likely be based on volume of sales rather than importance of a disease area. Research for conditions such as Parkinson's, Alzheimer's, osteoporosis, and ALS will all but vanish. Progress in remediation of other diseases, such as cancer, will fall off and the treatments we have now will be the only treatments available for the foreseeable future. Companies will focus more on unmet needs rather than improving already existing standard of care treatments, or they will turn their attention toward disease areas that have inexpensive development costs.

Malpractice insurance costs have often been cited as another source of high healthcare bills. These are pass through costs to the individual receiving care. That malpractice insurance costs have skyrocketed is more a testament to our litigious nature than the incompetence of the care givers. While there are some inept caregivers, most are not. But many spend too much time and too much money defending themselves from, oftentimes, results that are beyond their control. It would be good to remind ourselves that treatment of the human condition is still in its infancy. We have had a steep learning curve over the past hundred years, but there is still much to learn. And even what we know is not formulaic; the same disease can present different symptoms, outcomes, and comorbidities in different people. Not all are predictable. We have to understand that caregivers act and provide treatment based on the data and experience they have, and they can't always foresee future consequences. There may be factors hidden or masked in any given situation. The more experienced a caregiver, the less likely that small things will elude a diagnosis. Naturally, we should expect satisfaction in the cases where negligence occurs; however, we should not prosecute for things that are clearly beyond control. Easier said than done, particularly if we are, in one way or another, directly affected. It's not at the same level as if someone made a mistake in fixing a TV. Healthcare deals with lives—the lives of people close to us, the lives of people for who we care. It is inevitable that Emotions run high, and when a tragedy—no matter how small—occurs during the course of treatment, we instinctively look for someone to hold responsible, someone to lash out against to vent our pain. More likely than not, it's the caregiver and more likely than not, it's in the form of a lawsuit. Malpractice costs will always contribute to higher costs. The only thing that can serve to reduce this aspect of healthcare cost is litigating for a purpose and not litigating to relieve Emotion. That begins with us, not with healthcare providers, insurance companies, or pharmaceutical/medical device companies.

Standard of care costs the same to everyone. Naturally, if an individual wants something beyond that, it runs a bit more. The problem is not everyone is equal in their ability to pay for that standard of care. The more an individual earns, the less of a burden it is. But still in our relatively well-off Society where the Gaussian curve for earnings is comparatively broad, even a simple treatment/procedure may have devastating consequences on a family's fortune. To offset that, we employ private insurance schemes. But the cost of insurance is measured by the perceived risk of the individual policyholder. The payment of claims, as with any insurance, always rests on the shoulders of those who rarely use the insurance. This is all well, fine, and good for something like automobile insurance, where a policyholder seldomly—if ever—needs a large settlement. But for healthcare costs, needing an insurance payment is far more common. A policyholder may use that to offset costs several times a year for minor or routine treatments and a number of times in their life for more serious conditions. Both those increase in frequency as we grow older. Consequently, insurance companies demand higher premiums, higher deductibles, or higher co-pays. As these premiums rise, the healthy among us—usually the younger Constituents—either elect to go uninsured or take policies that have the lowest premiums. This reduces the pool of cash an insurance company has to pay claims and so they respond by raising premiums. A vicious downward cycle is born. With claim payouts and age having an inverse relation—that is, the older we get the more healthcare we need—this creates a social stigma insofar as we, as a Society, empathize with the elderly and have a desire to provide for them in deference to their contributions in the maintenance and progression of Society. This stigma is only all the more aggravating when we consider we live in a Republic that is so well endowed with resources.

The knee-jerk reaction of Society is to throw this grenade into the lap of Government, demanding intervention and a solution. This only serves to complicate the issue. Under our Social Contract, the Government has no obligations other than the ones previous cited to remedy the situation. For Government to effectively respond to that demand would require Society to surrender more of its liberties and trust that Government has the resources and know-how to provide a system that meets the needs of all the Constituents. Moreover, it will actually need to commit those resources. Emotionally, it satisfies us: Someone else is going to take care of us and we needn't do anything. The buck has been passed and it's someone else's problem to solve. But the Government isn't our Mommy or Daddy, and it doesn't serve the interests of Society to cede any more liberties to Government than is absolutely necessary. As history has demonstrated, it is very difficult to take back something once given.

Involving Government in any issue tends to be the last act of a desperate society. There are several reasons why, in this case, we should resist the urge. First, any resources the Government would muster, by default, come from the Constituents. Government doesn't just print money when they need to spend it; there must be an accounting against a budget whereby funds are supplied through the collection of taxes. From the Constituents. The bottom line is that instead of paying private insurance companies, we are paying Government. That may not be a net-sum-zero game.

Secondly, if Government provides for healthcare services, Government will determine what is and what is not covered under a plan. Unlike private insurance companies where an individual can shop around for the services that best fits their needs, the level of care will be dictated by an organization to which there may be no appeal. Your body will no longer be under your control.

Consider how that would impact elective surgeries, alternative medical treatments, abortion, and anything outside what the Government defines in its plan. Socialized medicine has not been well received in our northern neighbors nor with our English cousins.

Thirdly, involving the Government has the possibility of destroying two of the Republic's largest business sectors: Insurance and pharmaceuticals. Aside from the loss of a vast number of jobs needed to support the functioning of these industries, the Government would lose a fairly significant tax base. A tax base that would need to be offset through new or increased taxation, a taxation that has the potential to trickle down to the individual Constituent. Moreover, if we need to help support the unemployed from these two giant industries, this Government solution suddenly gets very expensive.

Fourthly, a centralized Government healthcare system has the potential to be overly bureaucratic. Typical in these types of bureaucracies is the use of employees who are not necessarily experienced or qualified enough to provide the efficiencies that private organization can. Bureaucracy has, historically, served to increase costs and response time. This can be averted somewhat if some professionals dedicate their service time to this effort, but that only assumes that such a service program is in place. Which, presently, it is not. We already have real world examples of how this bureaucracy has added a level of complexity to government healthcare. So much so that our healthcare industry has profited. On the other hand, there are a number of examples where government healthcare works; however, we need to keep in mind that in those instances the Gaussian curve of income and people looks like a plateau: The bandwidth of the middle class is quite broad.

Since the Clinton Administration, Society has been continually blaming healthcare companies for high costs, and we have been, sadly, looking to Government for a solution, all to no avail. It is rather interesting that the parties that have the most to lose—insurance, healthcare providers, and pharmaceutical/medical device manufacturers—haven't banded together to provide some kind of commercial national healthcare program. It would seem like self-preservation: If they wait for Government to further legislate on this issue, it can only be to the detriment to those parties. We already see a move towards federal drug pricing as the next logical step. The next step after that will be the bundling of treatment into a single cost. This could be followed by raising the bar for drug/device approvals. Or limiting standard of care to only three marketed treatments in any given therapeutic space. Whatever the eventual solution, it will need to be a precarious balancing act if part of that remedy is to provide affordable healthcare and at the same time continue progress in finding and developing new and better therapeutic treatments.

The Republic is at a crossroads with healthcare. Once committed to a path, it will be very difficult to go back. As with any issue that lies beyond the scope of the Social Contract, it is best that the solution comes through Society's efforts rather than those of Government. Exploring a tiered billing scheme based on income (much like how we are levied taxes) or bundling all our different insurances into a single plan (so that, like retail, more profitable sectors can help cover the costs of the lesser profitable ones) may be a start. A solution does exist, but if Society as a whole is to retain a semblance of its liberties, that solution may be best served if a solution: (i) not be rushed to provide immediate and short-term gratification; and (ii) not be borne of Government initiatives.

On What is Life

One of the most divisive issues in our Society's relative recent history is abortion. At its core, it is relatively straightforward under our Social Contract. As long as performing an abortion does not have an impact on the liberties of another, the decision remains in the realm of an individual to have or not have one. To the extent that it does not impact safety, security, or infrastructure, it lies outside the purview of Government and so is not a beneficiary of Government resources. The contention arises when the liberties of others are perceived to be infringed. These allegations have been, traditionally, inconsistent to varying degrees. So muddied is the issue by special interest groups, the media, and the judiciary, that we see a host of differing and sometimes contradictory legislation between the Government of the State and the Government of the Republic. Examining these inconsistencies and putting the issue in context of our respective obligations under our Social Contract may help the debate arrive at some sort of détente, however uneasy.

It is helpful to first acknowledge that abortion is a consequence of sex wherein the female becomes unwantedly pregnant. That sex can either be consensual or forced. Putting aside non-consensual sex, wherein special considerations need to be made and is beyond the scope of this general discussion on the topic, consensual sex is a choice freely made by two people. It is a matter of a bi-party Responsibility. No one in today's Society can, in all good conscience, argue that the participants in sex have no idea of the potential outcomes of that act. Gone are the days where we sit our children down and explain to them the birds and bees. In truth, children are more likely to educate—or at least shock—parents. So, from a very young age, we have knowledge of the consequences of sexual intercourse and of knowledge of how to manage those consequences, wanted or unwanted. Pregnancy is a result of two people utilizing or not utilizing these methods to a degree successful or otherwise, as the case may be, and the responsibility of that pregnancy lies with them, not Society. As such, the choice of bringing that fetus to realization is limited to those two individuals and should have no bearing nor present any burden to the rest of Society. In the case of the pursuit of happiness gone awry, the Government has no part to play other than its obligation to ensure that any ensuing medical procedures are safe and lawful. More specifically, no Government financial resources should be diverted to the support or opposition of abortion. In this, it fulfills its obligation to provide safety.

Abortion is a fairly simple surgical procedure on par with removing an appendix or repairing a hernia. No one has an issue with the state of medical technology in that regard that *per se*. The banners are raised because of the effect of the surgery: It removes the potential for life of an organism. We fear being complicit in murder. Even so, a great deal of judicial verdicts has centered around the rights of individuals to have an abortion. Largely, the rationale to allow has been focused on preventing future social stigmas: Rising healthcare costs, crime, subsidizing single mothers, poverty. While these seem attractive and appeal to certain sensibilities—particularly to women who have to carry an unwanted fetus to term—they should rather be an affront to us. And oddly, our offense isn't that of assailing our values of life but rather it suggests that a certain portion of our Society is of an inferior caste incapable of managing their lives without the interference of Government.

As part of legalizing abortion in 1970, New York State leaned heavily on a 1966 study that looked at 188 women who were denied abortion between 1939 and 1941 in Gothenburg, Sweden. The children of these women "turned out to have been registered more often with psychiatric services, engaged in more antisocial and criminal behavior, and have been more dependent on public assistance" (Rockefeller Commission on Population and American Future). That this report weighed heavily in the decision to legislate cannot be readily dismissed: Rockefeller was a Republican governor in a state when, at that time, Republicans enjoyed control of both the Assembly and Senate. Of course, the irony here is that Republicans generally side with the anti-abortion camp.

In their 2001 paper, "The Impact of Legalized Abortion on Crime," Steven Levitt (University of Chicago) and John Donahue (Yale University) seemed to confirm the Swedish findings. They alleged that the decline in crime in the US in 1992 was due to the absence of unwanted children following the legalization of abortion in 1973. This report began an ongoing feud between Levitt/Donahue and John Lott/John Whitley over the interpretation of the data. So intense the disagreement, it lasts to this day. As any statistician will tell you, the data will tell you anything if you torture it long enough.

People are too unpredictable to be able to use one or two points of data to categorize their future behavior. Children, in particular, are blank sheets of paper on which their families and environment write. There has not as of yet been identified a gene for evil. So, we need to look to the generation that produces them if we are to prevent the social ills we are trying to avoid by abortion. If we side with the findings of the Rockefeller Commission and we agree that preventing the pregnancies of certain women will improve our social fabric, doesn't if follow that we should stratify those women who receive abortions to create a database wherein we could proactively identify the demographic that are most likely to produce offspring that will be undesirable additions to Society? And once identified, wouldn't it be more economical to eliminate their ability to reproduce rather than to eliminate their unborn offspring? We can all see where this is leading, and none of us want to go down that path. We spend a lot of time and effort trying to justify the legalization of the act of abortion in hopes of winning over, through logic, those opposed. This is largely unnecessary under our Social Contact. As long as abortion does not infringe the rights or liberties of another, it is solely the decision of the individual. Any moralistic influences are more appropriately done on an individual basis and within spheres of influence that begin with the family unit, however that is defined in each unique case.

The caveat is determining if abortion affects the rights or liberties of others and, if so, who. Naturally, the mother is involved. As is the father—up to half the genetic makeup of the fetus is his. Are the rights and liberties affected equally between the mother and father? Of course not. The physical burden, after conception, lies with the mother. But this is something we all know and understand. It's not a new concept. We can't countenance women who want to eliminate men from the equation completely. What they do—or don't do—has the possibility of affecting others. To what extent and how weighted the decisions are in the process, there is no formula. Each case will, indubitably, have its own parameters. If the father relinquishes his responsibilities, then we can say that his rights and liberties are unaffected by the decisions of the mother.

But we aren't talking about the removal of a gall bladder or an appendix. We are discussing the termination of a potential life form. As we deliberate over this, a plethora of factors start muddying the waters most of which are esoteric, Emotional, and religious. We start projecting our fears and beliefs on Society, rather than being content to manage those in our own spheres of influence. The value we most want to overwrite on the rest of Society in this debate is our thoughts on life.

But what is Life?

What we can be sure of, no matter which side of the issue we are on, is that, unless you are a madman, nobody wants to be a murderer. Aside from being unconscionable and Wrong, it is illegal. As murder is the willful taking of another's life, we need to be sure that we have an excruciatingly exact definition of life knitted into our Society's psyche if not at least in Law. Yet we find ourselves in exactly the opposite situation. Our definition remains quite broad: The period within which a plant or animal exists as a vibrant, growing, or even subsisting organism before it dies. As pertaining directly to humans: The state of being alive as a human; an individual's existence (Black's Law, 2014). What is vague in this context is not so much when life ends so much as when it begins. To add to this confusion, we see conflicting applications of this definition in our codifications: The Government of the Republic has enacted Laws that provide for double homicide for certain crimes under federal jurisdiction if a woman is killed while pregnant with a fetus at any stage of development (18 USC 1841; 10 UCMJ 22)—seemingly in the face of *Roe v. Wade*. The Government of the State may, in absence of such a qualifying jurisdiction, interpret the meaning and prosecution of double homicide under any circumstances as they see fit. The conclusion that we can draw from these inconsistencies is that there is not yet a unified sense of when life begins, a granularity that we ought to have in order to cement the values of our Society.

Determining whether life begins upon conception or upon birth or anywhere in between is not a decision to be undertaken with Emotion; it must rely on Compassion and include no certain nor small amount of biological science. Once defined, we must acknowledge that it is for the good of the Society, and that this clarification is a benefit in determining what is fair. What is Right in these situations, must be determined not by standards or Laws, but by the family values that pass from one generation to another and as are inherited and practiced by those persons affected in each individual case. In the end, not everyone may agree with the definition of life as determined by our duly elected representatives, but in the case of abortion, we may control that practice within our own spheres of influence through Right action, by taking responsibly for our actions, and through the support of our immediate circle of family and friends.

In the absence of determining when life begins—something that may prove impossible given our limited understanding of life in general—it may, instead, be more practical to determine when life is viable. "Viable," in this sense would mean the point at which a fetus, if removed at a particular stage of development, would, with the application of present-day technology, have an overwhelmingly good chance of continued development into a healthy, self-sustainable organism. This may prove difficult to quantify: What would be considered an "overwhelming good chance?" Furthermore, as technology grows, this may be a moving target. As Society's technological acumen grows, the mark may, theoretically, get closer and closer to conception. It would at least and for the foreseeable future, however, draw a clear line whereby women would remain in sole control of decisions relating to their bodies until the point where it is no longer just their body.

In the end, abortion is an act to erase poor judgement or to alleviate mental or physical dangers to a woman. In the former application, it can be construed as a means to escape responsibility for the actions of two consenting individuals. In this sense, it is fundamentally Wrong. It serves to provide a sense of relief and, in some cases, saves Reputation. That being said, nobody is 100%; we all are intentionally Wrong sometimes. In our Society, however, personal choices should not be subject to Government intervention unless they affect security, safety, or infrastructure. In this case, Government involvement extends to the assurance of safety in procedures, and in exacting an infrastructure in which Society's individual Constituents may weigh their options and arrive at a decision appropriate for their unique set of circumstances, which decision neither impacts or limits the liberties of the rest of Society.

The October 22, 1993 Departments of Labor, Health and Human Services, and Education, and Related Agencies Appropriations Act (1994) limits the use of federal funds for abortion to the endangerment of the life of the mother (originally part of the 1976 Hyde Amendment), rape, and incest. In other words, the Government of the Republic reinforces its role in our Society. It focuses resources on safety, security, and infrastructure. Unfortunately, the Government of the State does not always share in that focus. Sixteen States provide resources to subsidize abortion. The rationale is to provide an avenue of relief for low income women and to reduce the State's future financial burden in supporting a child, or children, of low-income women. In our Social Contract, there is no distinction or separation of obligations between the Government of the Republic or the Government of the State. Each provides the same but the former more globally and the latter more locally. No matter the reasons of the State, providing resources for abortion lies outside its purview and supplying resources in the face of that without the consent of the Contributing Constituency is a breach of our Social Contract.

Unfortunately, it's difficult to argue against the economics of abortion in low income women. The cost of an abortion is far, far less than the cost of raising a child. The cold, hard math supports the elimination of potential life rather than the support of life. And the math gets much better when we look at proactive costs rather than reactive ones; that is, the cost to prevent pregnancy. It's an attractive proposition—IF part of the Social Contact holds an obligation for Government to provide resources to those in its Constituency that are irresponsible in their obligations as a Contributing Constituent. But we don't live under such a Social Contract. We understand that all of us may fall down occasionally and need a hand up, but unlike unforeseen complications in an individual's life that may require the temporary receipt of extraordinary services by the Government, it would be difficult for Society to extend its Compassion to a situation that is virtually 100% preventable.

On Pandemics

Much of what we believe in life is determined by perspective. Is the glass half full or half empty? In that vein, when we look at our relationship with nature, our perception can lead us into a false sense of security. From our vantage point, we consider ourselves as masters of the Earth, occupying the top niche of the global biome. Every animal, mineral, and vegetable are subjected to our will; they all exist to serve our wants and needs. Or so we think. We take what we want, and use resources as we see fit, oftentimes without regard to the long-term impact it may have on us and the environment we rely so very much on for our future. If there are things that oppose us, we find solutions that eliminate or—failing that—subdue them. Part of this conquering has been a concentrated and overarching focus over the centuries to prolong our individual lives. The relatively great strides in achieving immortality have been typically made through our advances in medical sciences.

In particular, the last century has seen great advances in our understanding and application of medical science.

A good indicator of this is the increase in our life expectancy. In 1900, men lived an average of 46.3 years and women an average of 48.3 years. That rose to 66.6 for men and 73.1 for women in 1960 largely through the mass distribution of penicillin in 1945 along with the implementation of modern pharmaceutical drug screening methods which facilitated new therapies. In 2017, men enjoyed an average of about 76.1 years of life while women lived to about 81.1 years. While certain conditions, such as cancers, have proven resistant to our curative efforts, the advances in the treatment of diseases and the various cures we have found have convinced us that there is little we can't overcome, particularly with respect to transmittable diseases. Our so-called mastery of cellular biology insured that we would never again experience a wide spread, uncontrollable outbreak of a disease; in short, a pandemic. Our manipulation of biology gave us confidence that were we confronted with such a predicament we would be able to nip it in the bud.

As with anything, whenever you think you're doing enough and you're good, something comes around and knocks you on your ass. That's life's way of saying you're not good and you haven't done enough. Our approach to transmittable disease is no different. So it should come as no surprise that when a pandemic strikes, we are, more often than not, ill-prepared. In fact, we almost never see it coming. We ignore the warning signs and are dismissive of the coming storm clouds. Once we realize it's upon us, it's often all too late. This is not a failing in healthcare or therapeutic treatments, it's a failure to learn from history. Before the COVID-19 pandemic of 2020, we had experienced numerous, smaller, and more manageable opportunities from which we could have awakened from our egotistical slumber and from which we had a chance to chart out policies and draft measures needed to deal with a disease that rips through a society at a breakneck pace leaving a swath of death in its wake. But the end of each of these pandemics was met with relief and a sense of having escaped something terrible. That we had dodged this metaphorical bullet was chalked up to skill rather than to luck. So, we continued on thinking we were doing enough and we were good.

When COVID-19 hit America, it was a cacophony of confusion. At first, it was passed off as another type of flu. Yes, it'll affect the very young and very old, but most of us would escape its nastier effects. The virus would act like many other viruses and dissipate when the warmer, wetter weather of summer arrived. Then we found out why our leading infectious disease experts were calling it "novel." All that stuff wasn't quite true, and the disease seemed to defy characterization as it began to infect people of all ages at blinding speed. This was met with a wall of confusion and indecision. No one knew what to do or who was responsible for doing what. The great cry was that this was unexplored territory and we needed to figure it all out on the fly; we had never before encountered anything like this. But looking back, it wasn't completely new territory: Spanish Flu 1918 – 1919; Asian flu 1957 – 1958; H3N2 (avian flu A) 1968; HIV 1981; SARS 2002 – 2004; H1N1 2009; Ebola 2014 – 2016; Zika 2015 - 2016. With perhaps the exception of the Spanish Flu, most of these fell short of the grandiose scale of COVID-19; however, they were more than ample in scope to certainly provided us glimpses into the chinks in our armor were they to have escalated. Our failing was that, despite these cautionary tales, we wallowed in the emotional reliefs that near-misses instill and, wrongly, believed steadfastly that our technology was the savior.

Part of the problem may lie in the way we view these earlier outbreaks. Rather than treating them liking the training wheels we use as we learn to ride a bike, we may have interpreted those events as the worst that nature could throw at us in this modern age. But a pandemic, by its very definition, spreads like lightning through a population and indiscriminately strikes everyone in that populace. In this era where air travel makes any place in the world accessible within a matter of hours, diseases are no longer constrained by the physical barriers that traditionally contained them in the past. This intricate web of frequent travel makes difficult the prediction of when and where a disease may infiltrate a populace. Case-in-point: We all knew that the global COVID-19 outbreak began in China, and while we barricaded ourselves from air travel from that country, the virus slipped in through the large number of flights landing on the east coast from Europe. New York City was ravaged in a matter of weeks. Commuters and connecting flights quickly gave the virus opportunities all along the eastern seaboard as well as access deep into the Central Time Zone.

Dealing with diseases is like doing a crossword puzzle: You solve all the easy ones first. The difference between solving and not solving the puzzle boils down to a handful of difficult problems. We have, likely, conquered all the easy diseases, generally through vaccines. Some, like the common cold, still elude us. But what remains are the really nasty diseases with the really nasty effects. Like death. What differentiated the COVID-19 pandemic from many of its predecessors was the speed at which it was transferred from person to person, its ability to affect people who were not normally associated as being the most vulnerable, and the rapidity of its progression from onset to death. Had any of these factors been absent, events would've transpired much differently, and the virus would likely not have had such a prominent place in the history books.

What is odd as we stare out over the valley of our medical achievements and bask in the glory of our progress, is that when we look at how our Society coped with the Spanish Flu pandemic in 1918 and compare that to what advice our experts gave us to fight the coronavirus in 2020, the advice is exactly the same. Stay home if you can. Socially distance. Wear masks in public. Nothing really new in 100 years. Fairly easy and simple remedies. When it worked so well for us then, it is difficult to understand why our Society was so resistant to use those strategies in this century's context.

What is more perplexing was the resistance of Society to follow the guidance of leading infectious disease experts and the inability of the Government to provide consist and credible leadership. This pandemic has differed from all its predecessors in that the economic fallout seemed to have rivaled the physical hardship the disease wrought upon us. During the shutdowns experienced during the beginnings of COVID-19, it was often said that the cure was worse than the disease. Given that the disease meant death for some, one wonders how such a sentence could be uttered. If social quarantine was, indeed, worse than death, than shouldn't we all have logically chosen death as the better of the two options? Certainly, financial hardship is not a pleasant thing but one always has the opportunity to recover from that plight. Not so much so with death.

Looking at any pandemic through the prism of our Social Contract, responsibilities and obligations become a bit clearer. This allows for a better template when a society is designing a plan from which they can effectively mitigate the effects of a rapid spreading, large scale infectious disease. As Constituents, we expect that no one does anything that would infringe on the liberties of another. In this particular instance, it might be better to think of it from a different perspective: There are things an individual Constituent *must do* to ensure that they are not infringing on the liberties of others. These two statements may seem different or be chalked up to semantics, but they can be the same side of the coin. An individual doesn't drive on the left side of the road lest it impedes another individual's liberty to safely drive under the same set of traffic laws. That's what the individual *doesn't* do; what that individual *does* do is to drive on the right side of the road. The result is the same, but described in two fashions. Sometimes we need to do something to ensure that we don't infringe the liberties of others; it isn't always a passive effort. And while we can frame respective and particular responsibilities and obligations under our Social Contract—and there is merit in that—it all boils down to *doing* what's right.

In the confines of a pandemic, this proves more difficult than it might otherwise be. Perhaps the main reason for this is that doing what's right is not altogether intuitive in this case. Most of us think we have a basic knowledge of how viruses spread and what to expect when we are infected with one. Generally, we shrug the consequences off largely because most of us have only been exposed to mild to moderate viruses. Like the common cold. Like the flu. From these experiences we don't really perceive a threat to Society on the scale of a culling of population. We, to some extent, acknowledge that the very old and the very young are more susceptible to the effects a virus brings, but we rarely do anything to act upon that acknowledgement. Very few, if any, of us have lived through a time when a disease so relentlessly ravaged the world as did the Spanish flu or COVID-19. When those types of crisis hit a society, the common person is often lacking the scientific toolbox from which they might draw to combat and repel such on onslaught.

And neither should they have. Under our Social Contract, that responsibility doesn't fall on the citizen. It falls on the Government. Protection from a regional or nationwide threat lies beyond the scope or the capacity of the individual. Only Government, through an access to massive resources that Society amply enables through its financial obligations, can marshal resources and deploy them without regard to geopolitical lines on a map. We see this in other facets of our Society beyond that of a pandemic. When criminals cross state lines, it becomes a federal matter. We look to the Federal Bureau of Investigation (FBI) to lead the efforts to bring justice. When commerce occurs across state lines, we rely on the Federal Trade Commission (FTC) to standardize and unify business practices. When disasters strike, we await the arrival of Federal Emergency Management Agency (FEMA) to provide relief. When we rely on drugs and drug safety, there is the Food and Drug Administration (FDA). The sphere of influence of the Government of the Republic far exceeds the sphere of influence of the Government of the State making it possible to tap resources in kind and quantity that are not available to a State. Likewise, the Government of the State has the same responsibility to its communities; that is, the Government of the State's sphere of influence extends far beyond that of a single community and so it can bring more resources to bear which would not otherwise be available to the community.

Perhaps the most compelling—and obvious—reason for the Government of the Republic to be the tip of the spear for any pandemic is to ensure an even and consistent response over the entirety of Society. As history has shown us, leaving responses to the Government of the State results in different criteria for everything from quarantine times to social distancing rules to re-opening. History has also shown us what happens when that is left unchecked: States that have managed to bring the disease under control are threatened by outbreaks in other states. A national plan ensures that no one region is adversely affected by another as regions may progress at different rates.

Just as Government is responsible to formulate, enact, and enforce a response to a pandemic, it is no less an obligation Society to comply with that response. This is particularly important when failure in compliance affects the whole more than the self. An individual may take as many risks to self as that individual wishes…unless it infringes on the liberties of others. If, in a pandemic scenario, an individual refuses to comply with the mandates of the Government, there are two social consequences: One to the individual; the other to Society. If the individual is unaffected by those actions, the pandemic is, to that individual, rendered a transient event and of no consequence. In that individual's mind, it could be relegated as a "non" event, perhaps even a fabricated one. What that individual chooses to ignore is that their non-compliance could infect others in Society in which those affected would manifest the disease thereby causing them personal suffering and causing the Republic to expend much needed—and potentially scarce—medical resources. If the individual is affected by their non-compliance, then not only does the individual suffer but Society bears that burden as well. The infected individual may have already spread the disease, and now resources will have to be brough to bear in an attempt to try to bring that individual back to health. More assets will need to be devoted to track down and potentially treat other individuals who may have been in contact with the infected one.

Despite this being a bit Darwinian in the sense that non-compliance presents Society an opportunity to cull its herd of people who are either ignorant or dismissive of our Social Contract, it is clear that those who disregard competent leadership and that leadership's scientific and data-driven recommendations are infringing on the liberties of others, are violating our Social Contract, and are contributing to propagation of a situation full of all kinds of suffering and hardships.

What muddies the waters is the introduction of social factors that lie outside a purely cold, hard math response to a pandemic. Economy. Socialization. Politics. While the response to a pandemic is grounded in science and data—which in and of themselves are sometimes hard to flesh out completely, especially at the onset of a breakout—these other social factors can evolve into eruptions of Emotion rather than a continuity of Reason. Putting the economy aside for the moment, socialization is an aspect of our humanity that defines us. Aristotle said man is by nature a social animal and anyone who is self-sufficient to the point where there is no need to interact with society is either a beast or a god. Since we are neither, we need to have some degree of social interaction. We need to engage other people if only to reassure ourselves "we are men dreaming we are butterflies and not butterflies dreaming we are men" (Zhuang, n.d.). In short, we need interaction with people to retain our sanity. Spending brief and limited periods of time without human interaction can sometimes be enjoyable, therapeutic even, but when these periods are open-ended or prolonged, the result for most of us is that our Reason and Rationality are eroded by that ever growing, ever present, and uncontainable demon, Emotion. We become intolerant of our too consistent surroundings and, like a whistle on a tea kettle, vent on anything and anyone in futile attempts to relieve the building pressure inside our psyches. To wit, the not-so-far-fetched joke: When shelter in place started in March 2020 in New York State one was challenged to become neither a July divorce statistic nor a contributor to a December baby boom.

Heaped on top of the social stress is a political anvil that brings untold pressure to an already panicky situation. In circumstances where the general welfare of Society is endangered, we expect the undivided focus of everyone in Government—at all levels—to be on the amelioration of all factors of that circumstance. We expect them to be prepared, have contingencies already in place, and to execute those plans without regard to the advancement of any personal or party agendas. The maximum effective range of touting the accomplishments of a person or party while a pandemic remains unresolved is zero meters. Amidst a crisis, no one cares where a pandemic comes from or how it inevitably arrived. The barn door's open. That analysis is something for an after-action review. What Society cares about is what steps the Government is taking today to eradicate the disease and protect its citizenry from a further escalation of infections. Any "look-at-me" pundits only served to increase the anxiety of an already overburdened Society.

When economic hardship enters the equation, all hell breaks loose. Our Society is a ladder society; there always will be a top and a bottom with groups of people occupying a number of different socio-economic rungs in between. Some of the rungs allow the occupier to create a hedge against economic distress while others do not. In our Society, the majority of Constituents are generally one or two paychecks from being homeless. This can be a result of an inability of an individual to make wages that could enable the creation of a financial buffer or it could be related to the decisions the individual makes as to quality and quantity of life. At the end of the day, it doesn't matter except that if one has resources to carry them through the crisis, it serves to lessen the burden on Society both in the immediate sense and the future one: Fewer financial resources will need to be diverted during the crisis to maintain the Society, and less will need to borrowed against the earnings of Society in the future.

They say that when someone is experiencing pain from several different parts of their body, they only perceive the worst one. This analogy can be seamlessly overlaid onto our pandemic scenario. Faced with economic hardship and the threat of a disease, we react to the one that is worse. If we are not physically suffering from the disease, the threat is *de minimis* and we only feel economic pain. And *vice versa*: The possibility of death makes economic hardship pale in comparison.

A well-constructed plan by the Government should chart the extent its response has economically on Society in general and the impact on the individual Constituent in particular. Easy to say, much more difficult to do. With so many considerations—some seemingly at odds with others—it is like juggling chainsaws. Priorities can sometimes be blurred. Do we prioritize the individual at the cost of the corporations that we hope will recover and keep those individuals employed? Do we ignore the administrative needs of state and local governments who have been crippled by income loss but through who we still expect to provide services that are needed to pull us through the crisis? Through all these allocations, how do we hedge against an open-ended scenario? What is the balance between fiscal borrowing and ability of Society to re-pay those debts? In this, there are no easy answers, but the dire consequences of not having any answers at all seems to be an endorsement for Government to engage in an apolitical, cross-aisle confab. If there were any situation where all duly elected officials should hold hands and dance around the campfire singing *Kumbaya*, this would be it.

A coordinated, consistent, and even response by the Government manages expectations and allows for regions to progress through the pandemic at different paces. By not condemning the little affected regions to the same Draconian restrictions as the heaviest affected regions, parts of the economy can stay vibrant and viable. It sets up a fair standard for allocation of limited resources. It also provides for a win-win situation: The individual Constituent can continue with their livelihoods, and the Government can reduce the financial resources it may have to allocate within the Republic to ease the economic fallout of a shutdown. But it is incumbent upon the Government of the Republic to determine these areas since only it has the ability to oversee these regions which can extend beyond state borders.

Understanding the roles and obligations both of the Government and of Society in a pandemic helps everyone move through the various crises that are endemic to a pandemic. Beyond complying with these obligations and the response managed by Government, it can be helpful to Society to understand just why any restrictions and mandates are employed. We tend to assume that it is to keep the death rate low. Or by complying with these mandates and restrictions, the disease will disappear on its own.

Not completely true.

At the core of any pandemic and its resultant severity on a society is the depth of that society's healthcare assets. Predominantly that translates into hospital space, number of healthcare workers, and availability of medical supplies. If those factors are sufficient to absorb the number of affected people, then we hear little about the impact of the pandemic and the issues rises to little more than a page three article in newsprint, taking a backseat to whatever debate the politics of the day has sparked. This is what we have seen with some—if not most—of the outbreaks since the Spanish Flu pandemic.

Hospitals are limited by the number of their beds. Under normal circumstances, the average occupancy rate among all those beds runs around 65%; more (73%) for larger hospitals, less (43%) for smaller ones (Health, United States, 2017). In a pandemic where the disease unleashes life-threatening effects, the bed space that concerns us the most is how many Intensive Care Unit (ICU) beds a facility has and what is the typical occupancy of those units. There are approximately

92,000 ICU beds across the country. This represents about 15% of total bed space. On any given day, these beds are about 68% occupied (Halpern, 2015). This is a vital and critical statistic: It represents a number of people that, at any given time, are afflicted with some condition that will require the unique and specialized equipment and care of an ICU.

That leaves about 29,500 open beds. Nationwide. The thing to bear in mind here is that number is not distributed evenly across all the states. More densely populated regions—inner cities in particular—will see a higher occupancy rate than rural ones, even when taking into consideration the density of ICUs. One can see how small a buffer zone that is when we are looking out over a population of 320 million souls. Once these beds—and any others in a facility that can be used as an ICU bed—are at capacity, difficult decisions need to be made. The elephant in the room here is: Who decides who gets a bed? In crises, a medical facility will use a triage system to determine the best use of assets compared with the victims that are most likely to survive. Tacitly built into that system is the decision on who will live and who will die.

When a pandemic reaches the point where it is threatening to overwhelm available healthcare facilities, Society and Government are faced with the dilemma of deciding what to do from two different points of view: Either from a numbers game analysis or from a Compassionate one. Historically, only about 20% of a population is affected by a virus to the point of needing medical intervention; the remaining 80% get through it with mild, moderate, or no effects. Of that 20%, only around 3.5% cases will be fatal. Cold hard math puts that at less than 1% of the total population. Statistically, that falls well in the realm of acceptable loss. Think about investing in something that has a 1% chance of failure. Most would say the risk is well worth taking. Many surgeries have greater risks. In the context of a pandemic, this number seems to minimize the situation and we would wonder why all the fuss.

But this number represents a hypothetical death toll and then only as it relates to the disease. What we fail to see when we employ this type of logic is the number of deaths unrelated to the disease that could have been prevented but for the want of medical supplies and facilities. If a medical facility has reached its capacity and in comes a car crash victim, what do they do? What about the heart attack or stroke victim? What about the cancer patient that has had to have treatment suspended? Aside from the dramatic, what about the stent surgery candidate who codes out waiting for the end of an elective surgery moratorium? The bottom line is someone is going to die, but who? The other question we need to ask in face of this seemingly low number is, "Did anyone die because others infringed on that individual's liberties?" Certainly, actions that deny a person life is the greatest infringement of liberty one can imagine.

Like any other crisis, the severity of a pandemic depends on our preparedness and response to it. Both Society and Government have their parts, and if we are to minimize the damage a virus can do to Society, both must be diligent in fulfilling their obligations. The worst case is when the Government of the Republic fails to provide leadership and it falls to more local Governments to coordinate amongst themselves a response. In this, regional policies will dictate those responses and serve to isolate "coalitions" until a fragmented Republic eventually emerges. Society, too, will fracture resulting in the formation of "sub-Republics" and, if allowed unchecked, into a number of Republics where before there was only one.

But make no mistake: The success of polices in combating a pandemic lies with Society and its individual Constituents. Without compliance—no matter how seemingly onerous—nothing happens. Yes, like the plague, smallpox, measles, and Spanish Flu, a pandemic will pass. That happens one of three ways: herd immunity, a vaccine, or a mutation of the virus that renders it impotent. But there are costs: Lives, time, and money. All these take their toll, and it can be difficult for a Society to recover in the near-term. Amid these hardships, doing what's right never seems harder, and is a true test of our commitment to the Social Contact.

On Protests

The birth of our Republic and its Society was a troubled one. While the original colonies were united in wanting to be free of the tyranny of England, they were united in very little else. Following the surrender at Yorktown, everyone pretty much went their own separate ways. A type of government was formed but it was more for providing a measure of security than anything else. The Articles of Confederation, inheriting a debt-ridden republic and without the power to raise money, provided for a very silent national government and enabled the states to chaotically act independently of one another. A more organized modern-day analogy of that would be what we see as the European Union. It took more than 12 years from our declaration of independence and one failed government before we finally and miraculously arrived at a government that would serve as the legitimate beginning of the Republic. And this was only possible by acquiescing to the pressure brought to bear by some states who insisted upon a list of rights for the citizenry. The negotiated list, a more or less mirror of the Virginia Declaration of Rights, compromises the first ten amendments to the Constitution. We call them the Bill of Rights.

The very first of these amendments provides for protecting rights of expression by individuals *viz.* Religion, Speech, and Press. Also in that first amendment is a mechanism whereby the people may redress grievances they may have with the Government. The language used with respect to the latter of these rights leaves little to the imagination and, for a document written in the late 18th century, is wonderfully lacking in verbosity. It simply states, "Congress shall make no law…abridging…the right of the people peaceably to assemble, and to petition the Government for a redress of grievances." As we read this and apply it to our modern era, we should keep some things in mind.

First, the Constitution was pieced together to try to move us from a cluster of sovereign states into a nation. A Republic. The four most responsible for pushing this through—Madison, Hamilton, Jay and Washington—never thought of it as an enduring document; that is, they believed that at some point in their not-too-distant future when more time and more dialogue was practical, this would be replaced by a document that better framed our Society. Second, the addition of a bill of rights was a prerequisite by some states before they would ratify the Constitution. At the beginning of the process, there were, by some accounts, 124 different amendments comprising that bill of rights. This was pared down to the "secular Ten Commandments" (Ellis, 2015) we have today. During that process, Madison tried to be as succinct as he could more in an attempt to keep the process moving forward rather than crafting more comprehensive and prosy amendments that would inevitably generate endless debate. Third, a public assembly of people in those days was neither a great nor overwhelming number. Modern communication devices—the telephone, television, radio and internet—were ostensibly absent thus making the organization and attendance of gatherings a bit challenging compared to what we see today. In the days where a letter took three weeks to get from Boston to Philadelphia, people relied on newsprint wherein a story describing any given event could already be several weeks, if not months, old. Timely redresses to events was difficult on a local scale and nearly impossible on a national one. Moreover, the people of the time rarely had the free time to participate in such assemblies. Finally, after eight years of war, the people had enough of confrontation and more than anything wanted to get on with the task of rebuilding their lives.

But the framework which these gentlemen put into motion was so well received that rather than making efforts to re-structure, the States found that amending the Constitution was the preferable path forward. So, our First Amendment rights have remained intact and unchanged for over 200 years. Judicial challenges may have set precedents in how we have come to interpret them, but, by and large, they are as they read.

What we have seen over the years is a more interconnected, focused desire to assemble, and a more vocal desire to make known to the powers that be that certain segments of Society are dissatisfied with certain polices. What seems to have been lost is the idea of "peaceable." Too many times an assembly is more a mob than a vehicle to redress grievances. Even when an assembly starts peaceably, all too often segments of that assembly or infiltrators of that assembly embark on destruction and violence. The result: Looting, property damage, injuries, and the inevitable police reaction of tear gas, batons, and rubber bullets. The consequence of such gatherings is that neither Society nor the Government have come any closer to redressing grievances. Those issues are buried under the rubble and the outcry of violence from both sides. We can be fairly confident that this is not the mechanism that was originally contemplated in our First Amendment.

The failure of protests to achieve their ends—that is, to gain the attention of the Government to reconsider policies—cannot be singly attributed to one side of the protest line or the other. Each has its role under our Social Contract and in those roles, each has its own responsibilities. The foremost of these responsibilities is to maintain order and to prevent the anarchy and chaos that can ensue. There is nothing so defeatist in changing policy as a protest that gets out of control. Protests are meant to be seen and heard, not felt. Those that careen off the tracks and, oftentimes, destroy the very segments of the populace they want to help, effectively end any chance of constructive dialogue as focus shifts to the local economies that are wracked by unintended consequences. It will be those issues and not the original grievances that will occupy Society's mind. And those economic effects will be felt by Society as it will be the Constituents of Society who are tasked, through taxes, to support the injured and rebuild whatever destruction came out of a not-so-peaceable gathering.

Someone from both sides needs to be responsible. From Government, actions at a protest are monitored by local law enforcement and so it follows that the head of that agency—commonly the police commissioner or police chief—is ultimately responsible for the actions of the representatives of that agency. This does not, however, excuse the individual agents. They are bound by oath and duty to provide for safety and security of Society. In the particular case of an assembly, they can be viewed as Society's proxy which represents the balance of Society who either disagree with the assemblers or are concerned with preventing a chaotic or destructive situation whose results may restrict their liberties or be a future burden on Society. To these agents, when they are diligently performing their duties, one must deliver the same respect and courtesy as one would expect to receive from any individual in Society.

Naturally, the question always arises about the necessity and application of the use of force in assemblies. We expect our law enforcement agents to be well-trained and well-disciplined beyond that of the average citizen in responses to situations that would cause consternation across normal Society. We expect them to show restraint in circumstances in which we would find difficulty doing the same. What we do not expect is that they be martyrs or that we rob from them the ability to defend themselves in the face of imminent danger. If both sides are living up to their obligations, this case never arises. If, however, the assembly from the agents' perspective is breaking violent or there is evident destruction of property or if the predetermined boundaries of the assembly are being violated, these heavily outnumbered agents will need to take action. What actions they take and to what extent are largely determined on a case-by-case basis and according to what resources they have on hand. The standards for response and for escalation should be clear to both sides prior to an assembly.

Which brings us to Society's responsibilities. The first and foremost is to remain peaceably assembled. If this cannot be achieved or maintained throughout the assembly, then it can no longer be considered an assembly protected under the First Amendment and it will more likely be deemed a riot and a criminal act. In attempts to ensure the peace during these assemblies, many municipalities require that the assembly be registered and that the organizers provide a person who will take responsibility for the assembly. Dates, times, and places also need to be provided so that the rest of Society can be aware of any disruptions of infrastructure that would otherwise violate their liberties. If a citizen needs to go to a municipal building for some service, or needs to travel down some street for some purpose they should know in advance if that is not possible due to an assembly that blocks access to those public buildings or infrastructure.

There is resistance to this type of registration. First, it seems to restrict the spontaneity in assembling. Second, no one wants to take that kind of responsibility because, in truth, there is no way to guarantee the behavior of each and every attendee. Despite these objections, an argument can be made for such a system based on the failed results of so many assemblies in the past. For safety and security—even unto the assemblers—it makes sense. It allows Government to allot the resources that may be needed not only in terms of law enforcement assets but other emergency services as well. Medical and fire teams should be alerted not only in the unlikely event of escalation into violence, but for the simple reason that, in crowds, people may faint or become ill and that various and unforeseen accidents still happen. Moreover, in such organized assemblies, boundary lines are drawn *a priori* making it easier for both sides to respect those lines and, in doing so, ensure a peaceable assembly. Furthermore, should violence break out, the scope of destruction will be relatively contained.

But what see, more often than not, is a spontaneous gathering fueled by Emotion and all too often lacking a requisite amount of Reason and, by extension, strategy. There is no single person or entity to which Society can point and say, "That person is responsible." No boundaries have been established so neither side understands where is "too far." In these assemblies there is a fine albeit very vague line between a peaceable assembly and a mob.

Ironically, in gatherings that are redressing grievances in liberties, little thought is given to the disruption of liberties for those in Society who are adversely affected by the assembly. When public streets are blockaded, when public parks are overrun, or when public buildings are assailed and access denied, the assemblers have conveniently disregarded the Social Contract for their own means while at the same time making a show to wave that contract overhead to gain their ends. Again, the symptom most feared in a spontaneous assembly is Emotion. Emotion lends itself to disorganization; disorganization leads unfailingly to chaos; chaos births anarchy; and anarchy cannot help but to rage violence and destruction in its wake.

In either type of assembly—an organized one or a spontaneous one—the two pillars of maintaining both individual obligations under the Social Contract and elements for an impactful, peaceable assembly are Reason and self-policing. Use of Reason cannot be understated. We can see this in our everyday life. If we engage in dialogue with someone and they become more and more Emotional and less and less Reasonable, we dismiss them and their arguments out of hand. We cease to listen and are not likely to re-engage them on the same subject matter again. In short, they become nonentities on the issue. If, on the other hand, we engage in a dialogue with someone that exhibits a calm and level demeaner and employs Reason in arguments, though we may still yet disagree, we don't end the dialogue. Rather we look at the debate as a social challenge and work towards a unique solution that benefits both sides.

Self-policing separates the pros from the amateurs; the trustworthy from the untrustworthy; the faithful from the faithless. When we stand in an assembly and are subjected to unjustified actions or we observe such actions by any law enforcement agent, it is our expectation that such wrong action be immediately and decisively arrested by other law enforcement agents.

Likewise, the same self-policing behavior is expected from the assemblers. Assemblers engaged in looting, violence, and destruction should be identified and, if they cannot be contained by other assemblers, referred to law enforcement agents. In this modern era, identification and documentation of such incidences on either side has been made exceedingly simple through the use of cell phone cameras. In the end, though, the only tools needed for self-policing are moral courage, integrity, and the desire to do what is right.

Peaceable assemblies work. If for no other reason than there is no distraction to its cause. Nothing supplants the "Why" of the assembly. One can assert that assemblers that contribute to social unrest are not friends of the assembly at all, but seek to sabotage it. Whether we are protesters, assemblers, law enforcement agents, the media, or citizens looking on, leaning on our obligations under our Social Contract in whichever role we have ensures an outcome that builds on our Society and takes us ever closer to the perfect union our forefathers spoke so prophetically about. A Society where everyone does what's right.

On the Environment

A certain man has 365 pennies in a piggy bank. He spends a penny a day. Soon he realizes that half the pennies are gone. Knowing that the piggy bank—and by extension his ability to live—will be depleted in six months, he cuts his rate of spending to a penny every other day. That extends him another six months but that reduces his quality of living. After a time, he sees that he's down to 90 pennies. He slows his spending further to a penny every four days. Once again, he has added six months but has further eroded his quality of living. He repeats this process over and over again until he reaches a point where he has a few pennies but cannot survive.

The obvious bottom line is that given finite resources and the need to expend it, eventually—and despite every effort to conserve that resource—it will eventually be depleted. Nothing left. Such is the state of our Earth. Humankind, through its ingenuity, has used and transformed raw materials found in our environment into products that provide for a better and more comfortable life. Many of these goods we cannot imagine being without: fuel for cars; rare earth elements for computers and batteries; oil for plastic and synthetics; and iron, aluminum, copper, nickel, and zinc for machines, structures and tools. Yet, one thing is certain: Whatever is contained in the Earth is all we have. As much as some would like to believe, the Earth is not a living organism capable of spontaneously making more of these elements. The foregone conclusion is that at some point in the history of humankind either these resources will be gone forever or we will have depleted them to such a point where we will have lost the technical prowess to make use of them.

Technology and prosperity dictate how quickly we deplete these resources. As technology grows, more and more goods are designed and manufactured to ease various aspects of our lives and to entertain us in the free time that better efficiencies provide. As our financial situations improve, so does our ability to acquire unnecessary peripherals. We consume. And in our Society, the propensity to consume is born of an underlying fear of destitution. Surrounding ourselves with things imparts to us a feeling of comfort and security. So, the more we have, the better we feel. What we don't consider in times of plenty is the finiteness of our environment. Only when we are already in the arms of crisis do we realize our dilemma and feebly try to stir ourselves to action. Generally, it's too late.

There is no separating the use of resources from the evolution of humankind. If we do not make use of the elements around us, we would be a stagnant Society reconciled to an existence of loincloths scratching to survive on dirt and plants. Our ingenuity has propelled us through ages that are, ironically, named for the resources on which we most rely: the Bronze Age; the Iron Age; the Nuclear Age. As with the man in our example above, we, too, have been spending our pennies but instead of decreasing that rate of expenditure, we are accelerating it. We have only recently awoken to the plight this expense suggests. Oddly, our enlightenment hasn't been from the procuring of raw materials but from rather from the other end: Disposing of finished materials. Garbage. We are running out of places to cache our no longer needed/wanted manufactured goods. We are seeing that some of these goods stubbornly refuse to decompose, at least into earth- and human-friendly components. Many are inert or are transformed into poisons that infect water and soil supplies. The former takes up space; the latter inevitable finds its way back into the food chain wreaking havoc among countless species not the least of which is us humans.

We turn to the god of technology and put the shoulder of blame on him. But technology in and of itself is neither inherently good nor bad. Those monikers are reserved for those who use or abuse it, as the case may be. When we proceed at a breakneck speed down the technological highway with no regard for where we are or where we are going or what consequences may eventually confront us smacks of irresponsibility. In these times, we consume so much in the research, development, and manufacturing of goods only to have, in months, that whole process rendered antiquated by the next newer, bigger and better research, development, and manufacturing process. And no sooner than that ramps up into full scale production than it, too, is tossed into the trash heap in favor of the next biggest and best thing. Repeat *ad nauseam ad infinitum.* We find no better examples of this obsolescence than in the computer, television, or cellular phone industries.

The scale of production and use even of apparently small items translates into a quite significant consumption of materials. Of most concern are the rare earth elements that makes all these things possible. Although rare earth elements traditionally have referred to the group of seventeen elements (the lanthanides plus scandium and yttrium) in the periodic table, we can also begin to add to that list elements that occur in more abundance but that are increasingly being more difficult to source; *e.g.*, gold, silver, titanium, platinum, lithium, nickel. Without these elements, motors, batteries, computer components, solar panels, and wind turbines cannot be produced.

The answer, many will say, is recycling. To a certain, limited extent, that is effective, but only in that it serves to stem the bleeding of these elements out of our world; it does not prevent it. Presently, any recycling undertaking needs to be economic in two ways: First, it needs to be a profitable enterprise; second, the materials recovered need to outweigh the materials expended. No one is willing to undertake recycling activities if the goods they recover are not worth more than the resources and process needed to reclaim those goods. Only Government through the use of fiscal resources originating from the Contributing Constituency would be able to sustain an operation that perpetually runs at a loss. Presently, many of the recycling processes are labor intensive and still reject a large portion of the materials entering the process making the recovery of raw materials somewhat less than impressive. Few companies can embark on recycling to an adequate economically efficient degree. Consequently, the lion's share is being done, sadly, outside the Republic, predominantly in China. Two major culprits of this outsourcing paradigm are labor costs and lax regulations in disposing of the toxic by-products of the recycling processes. And so, we rely on a foreign entity to make us feel good about our ecological stewardship—or lack of it. Ecological concerns, however, do not drive that relationship, rather it is trade policies, exchange rates, and labor costs. In short: Economics. In these days of global economic posturing, particularly between China and America, our "greenness" vacillates in lock-step with that relationship. In one moment, the items we end users earmark for recycling find their way back into the market while in the next—and sometimes unbeknownst to us—they end up in a landfill or the ocean. From whatever precipice we wish to observe, we can all see this is far from a sustainable and practicable solution.

Recycling is not a perpetual process; that is; resources in do not equal resources out. Resources are expended. The most obvious is energy. Other losses include chemicals, maintenance materials that enable the process, and transfer loss in the process. These all represent costs and serve to deplete whatever of these resources are needed to recover the end product. From an engineering point of view, it is implausible to create a process wherein a product produced has less empirical value than the elements needed to produce it. Neither is it economical. It may be an optic we wish to project—recycling used things into new things—but despite the public relations boost this may confer, it still remains unfeasible. We do not expend gold to re-constitute a plastic bottle. We do not expend gallons of petroleum to change a newspaper into a roll of toilet paper. Saving on one resource while disproportionately expending another has little value in a common context. Moreover, it adds to the self-same problem we are trying address: Depletion of resources. Recycling will, naturally, be prioritized based on the abundance of resources both involved with the process and with the desired recovery; however, it seems that it would defeat this endeavor if we slowed the consumption of one resource only to escalate the depletion of another. It would be sensible, then, to always ensure a careful and well monitored balance between the two.

The recovery of certain elements which are essential to our present state of technology, while prudent, doesn't provide a sustainable path forward. In any process, there is loss. No metal is produced without loss of the element in the form of line loss, transfer loss, or slag loss. Recycling is no more efficient, particularly when considering the relatively small quantities of material. Recovering gold or platinum foil from computers can be achieved, but the heat required can vaporize ultra-thin pieces of any metallic material. Whether or not these problems can be solved with future technology is academic. We cannot do it now, so the unavoidable consequence is the continued depletion of those types of resources.

Now the first law of thermodynamics tells us that matter is conserved; these resources of which we speak are not actually "destroyed" in the sense that they cease to exist. They are merely in forms—and locations—that renders their recovery nearly impossible. There are some resources that remain in forms and in locations that permit us to reclaim them. While no resource can be truly called renewable (Second Law of Thermodynamics points to a future universal heat death where entropy is zero), we have typically considered resources renewable when they can be restored faster than humans can consume them. Air. Water. Sunlight. Plants. Historically, we have chosen to believe that such resources were, ironically, "evergreen" and would ever be at our disposal. This fiction was challenged when the human race exceeded the carrying capacity of the Earth. When we finally awoke to our reality, we found that, due to our sheer numbers, we burn these faster than Earth can replenish. And, as it turns out, these resources are the very same ones that keep us alive—not in luxury but in existence.

While some of these resources in some places are irrevocably lost, others can be recovered albeit at great expense in time, money, and people. Forests, that provide the oxygen we breath, can be regrown. Water can be purified and toxins removed. Air can be cleaned up. The ozone can be repaired. At the risk of personifying the world, we can see through our limited knowledge of physics and chemistry that the bodily functions of the Earth which renew these resources do not stop, they are merely outpaced by human consumption. The issue lies not with those processes *per se*, but in our far exceeding the tipping point which would allow that balance to continue. Unfortunately, the solution to this problem lies far beyond the walls of our Society. That being said however, as the far and away leading consumer in all resources, we find ourselves in a unique position to have a profound impact on restoring that balance by exercising good global leadership: Setting the example.

To wit, America has roughly 5% of the world's population but consumes 33% of the world's paper, 25% of the world's oil, 23% of the world's coal, 27% of the world's aluminum, and 19% of the world's copper. This comes as no surprise: While the America population increased by three times from 1900 to 1989, our consumption of raw materials over the same period increased 17-fold (Roddy and Moss, 2012). In 2017, the American primary energy consumption (including solar, wind, geothermal, hydroelectric, and biomass sources) was about 17% of the world primary energy consumption (US Energy Information Administration).

At first glance these figures seem staggering and it makes it hard not to condemn our Society for a disproportionate degree of opulence when compared to our international peers. But what rises in the shadow of these figures is a little something called "economy." Americans consume as much as they can afford to consume. Much of what we consume originates in other countries and some cases that consumption fuels their economies. In a way, their existence and prosperity depend on feeding our affluence. Without our consumption, their economies would be a fraction of what they are today with the consequence that their standard of living would be much less. Moreover, without their manufacturing with the intent to sell in America, our cost of goods would be severely impacted. We enjoy affordable products because they're not produced here. Likely the single driver in our ability to procure inexpensive goods is that foreign labor costs are so low; in many cases to the point of exploitation. Another factor is the nearly non-existent regulations with respect to worker safety and waste disposal. In true ironic fashion we condemn those practices but expect a supply of readily available products. On top of that, we refuse to produce those goods domestically either from the misguided belief that such work is beneath us or from our resistance to buying a domestically higher priced product over a cheaper, imported product. When one looks at this from a 10,000-foot perspective, we cannot help but to be entertained by the miserly application of our gluttony.

So, given the obligations under our Social Contract—both from the Constituent's point of view as well as that of the Government—how are we required to approach the use and consumption of resources? Of our environment? If there are obligations, are we too far down the rabbit hole as a species or will our Society's prospective measures influence the plight of the rest of the world?

As a citizen in our Society, we cannot embark on actions that infringe the liberties of our fellow citizens. Does our consumption of any product infringe on any liberties? The short answer is "No." Our lifestyles and their composite and respective balance of necessities and luxuries are determined first by our economic means, and, second, by our decisions. Insofar as we have the ability to use and discard products safely and according to whatever processes and regulations Government imposes for such use and disposal, we have no obligation to preserve or ration any resource that we may procure. This, to be sure, is not the answer for which many would hope.

The argument can be made that the perceived irresponsible use of resources and the immersion into extreme consumption of manufactured products infringes on the liberties of future generations. While this may seem so to some on an intuitive level, we must remember that liberty, in general, is freedom from arbitrary or undue restraint, especially by government, and that personal liberty, in particular, is the is the freedom to do as one pleases limited only by the government's right to regulate public health, safety, and welfare (Black's Law, 2014). There is nothing implicit or tacit in that which could be applied to the accumulation or possession of material items. Consequently, there lies no obligation by Society to conserve or ration resources of any kind.

If, on the other hand, we look at the issue from a Government perspective, we see things altogether differently. In its obligations to provide safety, security, and infrastructure in perpetuity, the Government must be vigilant in the use and disposal of every resource possessed by Society. It relies on an abundance—if not availability—of innumerable resources to develop, build, and maintain roads, bridges, electrical grids, communication systems, transportation systems, military equipment, and supplies of clean air and water. At the same time, Government also needs to safeguard Society from the toxins and destructive nature of certain wastes from entering into the air, water, and food chain. These provisos become more and more problematic as Society grows in population and shrinks in available open space. The effective solution to this resource puzzle, *vis-à-vis* the totality of our American response, becomes further muddled when we take into account the rate of growth, net resource usage, and overall reduction in arable land mass in the rest of the world.

A cursory glance at the situation leaves one with an overwhelming sensation of impending doom. It seems impossible to cease the depletion of our resources and, in that wake, the easy conclusion is that it would be useless to try. Despite this, there is an "X" factor we need to consider: We don't know the future. While technology has lent itself to the decimation of the planet, it could also be its savior. As of yet unknown processes, innovations, and discoveries that better enable us to manipulate our environment without destroying it may lie just ahead. We mustn't pigeonhole ourselves into believing that everything worth discovering has been discovered or that everything we know is all there is to know. Imagine if that was the case even twenty years ago. Where would we be today? As long as we remain curious about new possibilities, there is always the hope that we can evolve into a self-sustaining race that strikes a symbiotic balance with its host world.

The immediate issue is that these new discoveries are fueled mainly by economics and, to a much lesser extent, philanthropy. But mainly economics. People work on new and improved technologies through a desire to profit from them. As a consequence, those of us that are uniquely talented in the making of technologies available to Society are almost without exception snatched up by the industries which are most adept at developing and marketing them. The resultant competition to obtain a limited number of these high skilled workers and innovators drives up the price of retaining them. This sets Government, with its limited resources and various obligations, at a severe disadvantage. It cannot hope to bring in qualified individuals in the numbers it needs to address the very same problems that the private sector is looking to develop for profitability or, in the case of recycling and disposal, that the private sector has determined is decidedly unprofitable.

The motivation of corporations to pursue any business that have been heretofore unprofitable has typically been fueled by a need for a "hobby"; that is, a company is so successful that it can spare resources to explore solutions to other problems that have the potential to be lucrative if for no other reason than there is an unmet need and no one else is doing it. The problem facing our efforts with dealing with the environment is that it is not perceived as having a big upside. While the optics of such undertakings can be a public image coup, more gets in the way of actual solutions than may be worth the effort.

The solution to this reluctance by the private sector to solve environmental problem is not an easy one. Regulation is one route; however, regulation oftentimes requires legislation, and, as Hobbes accurately predicted, our duly elected representatives may skew towards what is economical rather than what is right. In this case, it is a genuine conflict. Is doing what is right for Society in the short term at odds with doing what's right for Society in the long term? As we sit here in our armchairs taking on a philosophical air, the answer is, of course, the long term. Sustainability, survivability, and evolution are ever preeminent factors in the mind—and existence—of a Society. But when we shorten the zoom lens and focus on today, we step back from that position and cringe at what it might cost us in our current lifestyles. When this reality hits us in the face like a splash of cold water, we, naturally, want to evade whatever pain the requisite changes may pose and gladly kick the can down the road to the next generation. The cold, hard math of it all is that some generation, at some time, will need to bear those changes. If we could exercise Compassion, we would understand that whatever needs to be done is best done when there is an abundance of resources that can serve to cushion the changes and ease us into a new lifestyle. Still, it would be difficult for any duly elected official to champion forced change on Society no matter how right it may be. In this sense, regulation would appear to be an undesirable path that, even if considered, should be a last resort.

As we have already mentioned, the only organization that can continually operate at a loss is Government. Its financial resources are, more or less (and with no small amount of irony), evergreen. And since it seems to be an obligation of Government to shepherd environmental resources under our Social Contract, it only follows that the solution to the problem is borne of Government. That, though, does not necessarily correlate to a Government operation. Since we have established that the most technologically skilled among us gravitate towards profit centers, it seems that all would be best served if Government would work together with industry in such a fashion as to incentivize the conservation and recovery of natural resources. If industry understands that money can be made in such a collaboration—or at least not lost, it may just spur the innovation we need. Government, though, needs to be cautious in its approach to avoid the wasteful spending reminiscent of past contracts. What we don't need are more $300 hammers. If both sides enter into a relationship from the position of doing what is equitable and right, it certainly is not stretch to say that, in our Republic at least, we can find a way forward that respects the liberties of the people and still provides for an open end to our existence.

And maybe, just maybe, the pennies do not necessarily need to run out.

On Special Considerations

What we have seen of late is that the only way to enter the nirvana of happiness is by requiring some special consideration from Society. At least that's what many believe. Unfortunately, the effects of these illusions have been to provide those extraordinary considerations at the expense of other segments of our Society. That expense is often in terms of financial resources or restrictions of liberties *vis-à-vis* quotas. One of the self-evident truths that we hold in our Society is "...that all men are created equal." As we have shown thus far, this does not mean equal in status, potential, wealth, or ability. It is a statement of equality under the Social Contract and under the Laws that Society may require of us from time to time. The founders of our Society were neither under the illusion that they had achieved equality nor were they certain that equality was even close to being realized. Nowhere is this more evident than in the preamble of our Constitution: "We the People of the United States, in Order to form a *more perfect* Union..." (italics added). It does not say, "We the

People of the United States, in Order to form a *perfect* Union…" (idem). They knew they were falling short—they were acutely aware of the many inequalities of their time—but they wanted to be sure that, as we evolved, this remained a goal of our Society.

And with that goal in mind—that is, to become more and more perfect, more and more equal—it seems to be counterintuitive to grant special considerations for certain segments within our Society. Rather, we should work to ensure that the existing fair standards and existing Laws are applied evenly to all and, working in that vein, redress any inequalities. The barrier to equality is, again, Emotion. We hold fast to some irrational preconceptions about a certain segment, and we feel the need to make them suffer or at least make them feel inferior to ourselves. When these preconceptions are stripped of their irrationality, we find at the heart of it, that we feel threatened by these segments and harbor a resentment that they may overtake us on the social ladder.

Resentment is something we really need to work hard at to eliminate from our Society. The underlying promise of our Republic is that through hard work, determination, and skill anyone can rise from the bottom of the ladder to the top. This has come to be known as the "American Dream" both here and abroad. We all aspire to it; some reach it, many don't. Those who don't attain it feel the urge to punish those that do. They want to penalize success. It seems strange considering that they are using the same social means to achieve the same ends. We can only, unfortunately and regrettably, conclude that this is a spiteful, Emotional response to their own shortcomings rather than a condemnation of another's success.

The media is riddled with examples of inequalities, mainly in the form of discrimination. The judiciary is troubled with making decisions on what constitutes discrimination and how to redress it. Landmark cases seem to reign in this process. But if we reflect on where we are in our evolution as a Society, use our obligations under our Social Contract as a sounding board, and remove Emotion from the equation, we all would invariably arrive at the conclusion that discrimination has no place in our Society and, if we stay strong in those reflections, discrimination should never occur.

A store or company selling products or providing services is not doing so for altruistic reasons; that business is trading its goods or services for either other goods or services or for financial consideration. *I.e.*, money. Beyond the ability of the customer to pay (and any other legalities), there can be no reason why that business should not sell their product to anyone. Since our Social Contract is between us as individuals and the rest of Society and not select segments of Society, they are obligated to sell to anyone unless there is a compelling and legal reason not to. The business, in establishing and engaging in commerce, is committing to doing that business with whoever has the means to procure the business's goods and services. If we were to allow for an arbitrary selection of customers—unless set by fair and consistent pricing—we automatically invite Emotion, the enemy of Right, to influence that selection. Furthermore, we summon our own personal biases and beliefs to control that Emotion. If we were to permit this Emotional filtering, instead of being a stalwart scion of whatever righteousness to which we think we cling or to which we wish to project, we merely end up as a foolish mockery of what our Social Contract demands. The only single and inescapable outcome is Wrong action.

As an example: In 2013, a Washington State florist refused to sell flowers to two men who were procuring them for their same-sex wedding. Invoking the First Amendment, the florist cited that this would violate the florist's religious beliefs. The Washington Supreme Court upheld a fine by a lower court and ruled in favor of the two men as the selling of floral arrangements did not condone homosexuality and thereby did not infringe on the store owner's First Amendment rights. The Court reviewed and affirmed their decision again in 2019 in the wake of the 2018 Supreme Court review of *Masterpiece Cakeshop, Ltd v. Colorado Civil Rights Commission*. In that, the Court reversed a decision rendered in this similar Lakewood, Colorado case due to the Colorado Commission's hostility towards the plaintiff's religious views leading to a failure of the Commission to exhibit an obligation of religious neutrality. Had the Commission fulfilled that obligation, the decision of the lower court would have been upheld. The final settlement of the Washington case took six years and took a convoluted judicial path. But if we look at this instance—or even the Colorado case—in terms of our Social Contract, the conclusion takes but a few seconds. The Washington shop owner projected personal beliefs—in this case religious ones—on a couple using the owner's business as a platform. The owner's obligations under our Social Contract are between the owner and the rest of Society, not just like-minded, religiously aligned segments. As the Court emphasized, selling goods or providing services is a function of business, not an endorsement, tacit or otherwise, of the use or provision of those goods or services.

Special considerations are, in part, a consequence of our spending too much time looking at the process and not enough time focusing on the result. There are instances where process is important—even critical (*e.g.*, defusing a bomb)—but, in general, for any decision that could be construed as discriminatory, the result should drive the process not the other way around. Looking at our previous example, what is the desired result: Selling flowers or spreading Christianity? If it is selling flowers, then refusing to sell flowers seems contradictory, almost inane. If it was the spreading of Christianity, why are flowers involved at all? Rather than a flower shop, a religious facility would be far more appropriate. In the more common instance where a person is hiring someone for a job, the employer is looking for the best person to perform the tasks associated with that job. At its core, the employer doesn't care who that is, what they believe, where they came from, or what they look like. It's cold, hard math: It's all about them performing the job to a standard. The employer knows what qualifications are needed to fill the position. That's the only concern. And the employer knows at the beginning how much compensation is available for that position. That number should not, absent negotiation or considerations in relevant qualifications or experience, change.

As one would expect, reality is the ultimate equalizer to imagination. We sometimes have dreams that when we try to translate them into our everyday lives find them lacking in the balance of reality. Limitations on abilities, monetary insufficiency, physical barriers, untraversable obstacles, social barriers, or just plain naïve thinking can all put a kibosh on an imagining. To most of us, this means making changes to our dreams so that they may be realized in, perhaps, a lesser form, or it may mean abandoning them altogether in the face of the impossible. Some of us, though, opt to ignore reality and prefer to bulldoze down a path that is rife with Emotionally twisted Reason. Under our Social Contract, they are welcome to do that provided that their pursuits don't interfere with the liberties of Society. But in the situation where they find that their perceptions are not founded or reflected in reality, then turning to Government for special considerations becomes their *modus operandi*. The fallout from such tactics has been confusion, inconvenience, strife, and infuriation.

Nowhere is this more pronounced than in self-actualization. As we have previously discussed, we are not what we think, we are what people perceive. These two can converge if we are successful in externalizing behavior that we believe we possess internally. But thinking we are one thing doesn't make it so; particularly, when there is external evidence to the contrary. The work-around for this has been the term "identify." This word is invoked by a person to imply that, overwhelming evidence to the contrary, the internal perception of self is the correct interpretation and the external perception observed by the rest of Society is in error. While we hear of all different variations to this theme—from identifying as a Martian to identifying as a different age—perhaps in no greater frequency do we hear "identify" used in the context of a man identifying as a woman or *vice versa*.

We do not determine sex on a case by case basis; in fact, we do not determine sex at all. That is a biological, genetically random determination made by the male's haploid cell (female haploid cells are always X-chromosome; males can be either X or Y). When a child is born, it is either male or female. This is a well understood result of the physical, chemical, and biological constraints by which life on our planet is subject. The lesser understood characteristic of life is the higher-level operation of the mind, or more exactly, how thoughts are formed. Why can we, as humans, think and reason to the point of using language, building cities, or describing the physical universe while other life forms on earth cannot. Science has speculation while religion offers other answers. But the fact is we don't really understand the entirety of it. One distinction worth making: When we speak of the mind, we are not speaking of the brain, we are speaking of the intangible consequences of brain function. A brain is an organ comprised of the same genetic makeup as the rest of the body. The two are not independent of one another. With this in mind, then, we unapologetically take a page from Rene Descartes's concept of substance dualism and consider a human lifeform as consisting of two components: the physical (cells, organs, neurons, etc.) and the mental (formation of thought, retention of information, reasoning capabilities, etc.) (Descartes, 1641).

When the body breaks or manifests a condition other than what we, through thousands of years of observation and hundreds of millions of data points, consider normal, we embark on treatment to restore the body to its normal state. Or as close to it as we can get. Medication, surgery, rehabilitation. Our goal is a return to normalcy. Even when we know there's no hope, as in cases of some cancers, we steadfastly continue in our endeavors to heal the body. We don't give up. When the mind breaks, we attempt the same thing albeit with lesser success. We treat depression. We treat schizophrenia. We treat bipolar disorders. We treat autism. We treat Post-Traumatic Stress Disorder (PTSD). We treat stress. We treat trauma. We don't accept that these conditions are natural states of a human even if such behavior manifests itself from birth. Yet when a person who is physically a male identifies himself as a female, we are expected to be complacent and accepting though there is clearly a dichotomy when comparing that condition to other mental states. Treatment is never something of which is spoken. Oddly, if a person were to identify themselves as a dog, or a cow, or a vampire, or a Martian, psychologists would be all over it.

We will not entertain the concept of a man trapped inside a woman's body or *vice versa.* This presupposes that there is a being that puts the essences of men and woman into bodies which by the very mentioning suggests a religious aspect, an aspect which is beyond our consideration under our Social Contract due to the practicing of multi-variegated religions within our Society. Moreover, were we to subscribe to this, then we would be forced to believe in a god that makes the simplest of mistakes or enjoys playing cruel jokes on its creation. Both are inconsistent with most concepts of god. What that leaves, then, is one of two things: Either the body is broken or the mind is broken. If the body is broken, then treatment should be accordingly, *e.g.*, hormone therapy. If the mind is broken, then that treatment, too, should follow accordingly; *e.g.*, psychotherapy.

Many will believe this an oversimplification. But what's left? And, again, this is not to say that Society restricts anyone from identifying as anything they want so long as that identification does not impact the liberties of others. When we find ourselves rearranging our Society around these identifications, we can be sure that a great number of liberties have been infringed to accommodate a minuscule segment of our Society. And this has an avalanche effect: Segment after segment—none wishing to be left out—will canvass for their own special carve outs of from what is usual and ordinary in Society until we have a myriad of standards so complex that would give even the most experienced attorney pause. In a society where exceptions outweigh the rule, the social contract has long since been forgotten and rather than a people living and evolving in relative harmony—or at the very least a tempered *laissez-faire*—we see its citizens fight each other for more and more special considerations. Our Society, while acknowledging that there will always be a certain number of social outliers, must not acquiesce to the demands of segments that would prefer Society to bend to their needs rather than address—and perhaps solve—the underlying problem at hand. The former is borne of privilege and frustration; the latter a child of a diligent exercise of the Social Contract.

Yet we already see signs of Society caving to the petitions of the outliers. There may be no greater example of this than the ongoing, never-ending debate about how to use public restrooms. Men who identify as women insist they be allowed to use the women's restroom; women who identify as men want to use the men's restroom. We needn't take the figurative ten thousand-foot view of the issue to see it more clearly, we merely need to visit another country. For all the rhetoric on that issue, the solution is not one that caters to who we think we are but what biology has dictated: Male equipment in the men's room; female equipment in the women's room. Like most other evolved societies on the planet. Let's not unnecessarily supplant simple common sense in favor of providing special accommodations that we hope make the issue disappear. The most obvious solution, of course, is unisex restrooms. The main inhibitor to that is Government would need to use resources taken from the Contributing Constituents to provide for these facilities in public buildings that already have adequate facilities.

"Providing Special Considerations" is the side B of "Redressing Inequalities." The slow path is to legislate *ad nauseam* in the belief that we can plug each and every hole and hope that such legislation will be enough of a stick to deter the Emotional among us from doing Wrong. This is an outside-in approach and assumes, again, that we as the Constituency are too feeble to do what is Right of our own accord. This assumption is neither acceptable nor tolerable under our Social Contract. If we were to drink from this cup, we would be lying down all our liberties at the feet of Hobbes' Leviathan. It is far more palatable to us as Americans to summon the courage and discipline to take an inside-out approach; that is, to muster the strength to put aside our Emotion and act with Compassion in doing Right in lieu of having mandates, dictates, and restrictions levied on us by a few all-powerful individuals.

Faced with the alternatives, we, as a Society, need to determine which approach is easier to swallow: the outside-in or the inside-out.

Mirror, Mirror…

We have looked at several aspects of our Society in the context of our Social Contract. We have looked at some of the challenges that have escalated and fractured our Society to a point where they threaten to plummet us into a Dark Age. We have begun to look at how to remediate some of these issues within the boundaries of our obligations to Society and the expectations we have of Government all of which preserve as many individual liberties as practicable. What we haven't examined is in to what our has Society evolved. Right is Right in every society, but it's cultural behavior within these confines that separates one society from another. So, what reflection do we see in the looking glass?

This isn't a new exercise for a society: Philosophers, artists, politicians, and clergymen have been writing about the ethos of societies and the heart of humankind for centuries. This is no less true in our relatively infantile Society. Thomas Paine. Mark Twain. Ralph Waldo Emerson. Henry David Thoreau. Walt Whitman. Ayn Rand. Leo Strauss. And too many more to mention. But perhaps the clearest and most concise insight may have come from Dean Brackley, SJ [Society of Jesus (more commonly known as the Jesuits)] . He mentions twelve characteristics of the world in which we live (Brackley, 1988), and it would appear, after scrutinizing these, that some paint a fairly honest picture of the American ethos as forged by two centuries of immigration and integration. Some are positive aspects; others are not. Using his observations as a foundation and paraphrasing some of his thoughts, we can summarize our Society and its cultural characteristic into nine qualities:

First: We are an individualized society. Our Social Contract is between ourselves and the rest of Society. We do not take on the burden of others under our covenants, but hold them responsible for their own. We, as individuals, confront the problems that present themselves in our lives: In relation to self (individuality and self-worth); in relation to nature (material needs); and in relation with others (the need to belong). We, whether strictly as individuals or by extension as a family unit, pursue private goals to meet all these needs.

Second: Our first instinct is to solve our insecurities by accumulating or consuming things. This may be a result of the underlying fear we have for abject poverty. By surrounding ourselves with material goods, we have a visual indication that we are not poor. The temptation is to take this too far and equate material accumulation with true wealth. This ignores the abstract and more enduring worth of a person. The elements of good character are qualities that cannot be bought at any price.

Trustworthiness, honesty, responsibility, reliability, sensibilities, morale courage, integrity. All are a measure of richness that endure long past the planned obsolescence of material things.

Third: We are a ladder society. Some of our members will have more worth than others. The higher up the ladder you are, the more worth you have. This reinforces our individuality, but serves to isolate ourselves from the rest of Society. We speak more of "them" rather than "us." In our Society, we have the ability to move either upwards or downwards on that ladder depending on ability, determination, education, decisions, and—sometimes—luck. We judge ourselves and others based on what rung we perceive them to be upon; particularly, whether they are above or below us.

Fourth: Status symbols determine one's position on the ladder. Some of these symbols are: job, type and size of house, type of car, vacations, beauty, skin color, social class, ethnic background, credit cards, and education (particularly, which school). Not only do these contribute to one's social position and the need to belong, but they define one's identity and sense of self-worth, most immediately to oneself. Strangely, the personal values upon which a person relies to determine his or her self-worth are not innate, but are provided by Society through several avenues such as parenting, government, media, schooling, church, and advertising. These sources tend to morph over time. Left unchecked—that is, without the application of Right—the character of our Society can be swayed by a relative few and in a direction that suits their purposes and not necessarily those that are in the best interests of the rest of Society.

Fifth: When Society, as a whole, reinforces and begins to dominate our environment, individuals interiorize this ladder model and project an associated pride. While pride, in and of itself, is not necessarily counterproductive to an individual or Society, there is a destructive type of pride that has the potential to be exhibited; that is, a socially arrogant one of being better than another. It makes sense that our worth is relative. It depends on what rung of the ladder we inhabit. It depends on who we perceive is above and below us. The more people below an individual, the more is that person's perceived worth. The all-too-often used method of rating one's worth is to what extent one has prevailing status symbols of the time. The danger lies in our own self-contempt *viz.* our attitudes at being worth less than others who are above us on the ladder. The exteriorization of these feelings can lead to the manifestation of inequality and unfairness to those above and a projection of hatred and discrimination to those below. The former is mainly harmless, the latter, though, is a cancer to Society the consequences of which are civil unrest, violence, and a breakdown of the society into strata, eventually giving way to extreme polarization.

Pride is the culprit, and if we posit that the beginning to character is honesty, then we can say that the depolarization of the society begins with humility. First examine what fault lies within and fix that rather than snipe at everyone else. Lay down the arrogance that has crept its way into our lives. Acknowledge what is real and what is Right. Understand and accept the ladder rung upon which we occupy and act in accordance with the associated character of that position.

Sixth: Every ladder has a top and a bottom. In our case it is the Model and the Outcast; the one with everything and the one with nothing. While in reality there are no discrete points for these, we do have ample examples for each. The movie stars, the playboys, the executives of big companies *vs.* the handicapped, the poor, the uneducated, or the ugly. In a competitive situation, we must all accept that there is a first and a last. That, in itself, is not a problem and is, in a way, a part of the natural environment in which we live. What matters is how we, as an evolved society, treat the one from the other. If one is with admiration and the other is with disdain, we have failed. As an evolved society, we cannot condone a system that condemns a person for who they are or what rung they occupy especially when the system we have agreed upon dictates that someone must occupy that position. If they are fulfilling their obligations under the Social Contract, they deserve no less respect than the individuals at the other end of the ladder. In fact, the increases in Responsibility that accompany movement up the ladder may not be all that enviable—or achievable—by everyone. In an evolved society, the greatest burden falls on the elite. They, in some fashion, control portions of society and are responsible to ensure that their acquisitions and accumulations are not gained by disadvantaging others, particularly those below them on the ladder. To exercise this great care is not something done casually nor without great effort.

Seventh: Competition drives our Society and, by extension, is at the heart of the Social Contract. Competition characterizes our social life and we are constantly reminded that someone lower than ourselves on the ladder can surpass us or take our position. At the same time, we aspire to raise ourselves and take someone else's position. This situation can easily be construed as threatening. If someone below usurps another's perceived material and social security it may affect self-worth. If people latch onto this, fear and mistrust can too quickly poison Society. Again, a pride of relative worth takes precedence over one's function in Society. We have seen how this fear and defensiveness has avalanched out of control such that we are now a people of attack dogs, pistols, and locked doors. The fear is, unfortunately, not altogether unwarranted. A failure in our Society has individuals trying to advance themselves through whatever means they have, oftentimes by violent means. The skewing of our values, of our character, and of what we attached to self-worth have led us to this precipice of isolation; an isolation of each individual in Society. The complication of Society can render us impotent to do what's Right. It's not that we don't know what that is, it's just that we are oftentimes too afraid to do it.

Eighth: Our self-esteem is linked with our upward mobility. Goals and success are measured by status and whatever symbols are the flavor of the day. Ambition and the drive for power fuel us. As long as responsibility, character, and a commitment to doing Right accompanies these urges, our Society can continue to grow and prosper. When these turn into a desire to control and inflict one's will upon others, a society turns its intent from building to tearing down; from moving forward to moving backward. As it is, most of us are content with a modicum of security. We may wish we were better off, but we are fairly happy with our lives. Unfortunately, in our legitimate search for this modest niche in life, the good people do not determine the rules of the ladder game. What we need to do is at the very crux of the social system we have chosen. We need to ever be vigilant about: (i) the dangers of the contest; (ii) knowing the whole and which part we play; and (iii) acknowledging that, even when we act in goodwill, we may risk serving social processes larger than ourselves and contrary to our positions. And here we need to acknowledge that, in every society, there is a mixture of Right and Wrong. When Wrong, even when in an overwhelming minority, overshadows and out shouts the Right, Society is tarnished and suffers and will continue to suffer until the proper perspective of Right *vs.* Wrong is restored.

Ninth: We have discussed a ladder paradigm, and this is useful to elucidate the different strata our Society; however, when we take into consideration a third dimension—the number of people who occupy the same, or nearly the same, strata—what we observe is more of a pyramid. People tend to band together with people of the same socio-economic-political caste. In this we form blocs and cliques and sundry other divisions. A certain power is associated with each of these divisions with some being stronger than others. Primarily, these divisions offer security to those in it; after all, we are social creatures and gravitate to those most like us.

This is who we are. This is our culture. We need to accept this and work within these confines or affect change through a cultural revolution that can spread to the farthest corners of our diverse ethnicities.

The Power of One

Everything seems much easier on paper. Architectural drawings, instruction manuals, troubleshooting guides, music, and, of course, philosophical treatises. We look at them and nod our heads in a kind of *faux* understanding fooling even ourselves into believing what we read and see is obvious to the point of being intuitive. Putting the simplest of them into practice, however, can be a completely different story. Reality, all too soon, snaps our heads back just in time to see our misguided naiveté come crashing down around us. Doing what is Right—as easy as that may sound—is no different. Maintaining objectivity in our Social Contract—as basic as that is—is no different. While these require strength of mind, strength of spirit, diligence, and plain old courage, none of them are qualities that lie beyond any of us. They cannot or we, as a culture, have embarked on a foolish path and are unwilling participants in a doomed experiment that can only—and logically—give way to an inevitable oligarchy ruled not by the most enlightened, but by the strongest, the most powerful, and the wealthiest.

So, where do these difficulties lie? First, Emotion is the largest natural predator of Right. The most common manifestation of Emotion in the failure to do Right is Want. Want is a feeling best described as an inconsolable need to possess something or an overwhelming, almost uncontrollable urge, to do—or not do—something. Want doesn't generally serve any constructive purpose, rather it incites anxiety and malcontent. If the host has the requisite discipline to properly channel Want, it can create motivation, inspire hard work, and instill focus. But that seems to be the exception rather than the rule. The source for a number of our ills stem from Want. Like some two- or three-year old caught in *Groundhog Day*, we find ourselves obsessively saying "I want…" or "don't want…" endlessly. These words are dictating what we do, how we do it, and to what lengths we go in doing (or not doing) something. They have turned us inside out, concerning us more with "me" than "us." They are the cause of disregard and lack of empathy which effectively threatens to turn a society of 350 million into 350 million societies. Want has nothing to do with doing Right except insofar as when—and if—it compels us to do Right.

Another stumbling block is when we interpret potential as promise. What ensues can be nothing but Wrong thought and Wrong action. In our Society, we are free to pursue whatever happiness we want as long as that pursuit does not infringe on the liberties of others. The potential for happiness is always there, but we are neither promised it nor is it conferred upon any of us. Perhaps

Benjamin Franklin is credited with saying it best, "The Constitution only gives people the right to pursue happiness. You have to catch it yourself." We have taken up the bad habit of defining our happiness in terms of the external and not the internal. We seek validation of our happiness through the envy—or sometimes the suffering—of others in our Society. If we would ever awaken from this self-induced coma, we would suddenly come to the realization that we are sadly devoid of the contentment and self-awareness that are integral to achieving the happiness we are so hopelessly pursuing in the first place.

In our struggle to restore our Social Contract *vis-à-vis* doing what is Right for ourselves and for our fellow Constituents, we first need to simplify the way we look at everything. Virtually every decision we make can be reduce to a binary one. We need only strip away the factors that we interject in any decision to bias the outcome. Once done, Reason needs to trump Emotion; Reality needs to prevail over Fantasy. This is not to say that we turn ourselves into Vulcans feeding on pure logic or some automaton with a decision engine for a brain. We are humans and possess no small amount of Compassion—that wonderful balance of tempered Emotion, empathy, and Reason—giving us the capacity to accomplish great things individually and collectively. When one considers the fundamental elements of any decision in the context of our Social Contract, a Right path will generally manifest itself. It is, then, up to the individual to either commit to following that Yellow Brick Road or, through a lack of moral courage or integrity, to willfully breach our Social Contract thereby becoming a pariah to all that we as a Society have worked so long and so hard to perfect.

Our contract is with Society, not each other. This proves to be too overwhelming to some in recent days. When visualizing the 350 million components that make up our Society, it can be easy to feel as insignificant as a grain of sand on the beach. We can fall into despair and convince ourselves that we do not matter; we cannot, individually and of ourselves, affect any change. As these feelings embed themselves into our psyche, we become numb to Society and relegate our role in it to that of a spectator. Sidelined, we watch neutered and paralyzed as life passes us by unaware of the power that we, as individuals, actual wield.

We have leaned too much on Government to chart our futures, and their happy response is to chip away at our liberties leaving us with fewer and fewer choices. Sadly, once ceded, these liberties are impossible to recover. They are forever gone. As Society has advanced, instead of reaffirming our Social Contract and reinforcing the wealth of freedoms it provides, it has increasingly become apathetic to the point of stagnation. As individuals, it is far easier and far less effort for us to acquiesce to a top down paradigm rather than a bottom up one. The consequence is that we look to Government to tell us what to do but then, inexplicably and incongruously, complain when they do. The ship is listing, and to right it requires each of us to re-familiarize ourselves with our Social Contract and then to re-program ourselves accordingly in order to return Society's power to its Contributing Constituency.

Previously, we discussed that every single number counts. We can't get to ten without the numbers one or five or seven or any in between. Each number, while perhaps having more factors than another, still carries the same weight and none is more important than the other. Take "1" away and the whole thing falls apart. Take "120,145" away and the whole thing falls apart. Choose a number; it doesn't matter. The number is irrelevant. Each has some position that ties it to another. What may not be so obvious is that when it comes to being part of a society a single number rarely stands alone. Each member possesses, to some extent, a sphere of influence. Like ripples in water, the closer in the sphere the individual, the stronger the influence. But influence obeys Newton's Gravitational Force Formula: As the influence radiates outwards it becomes exponentially weaker and weaker until it dissipates entirely. When we spend our time and energy in attempts to influence the farthest sphere without first strengthening the innermost ones, we inexorably meet with frustration and failure all the while wallowing in the throes of exhaustion.

We also have mentioned that if the individual is the element of Society, then family, however we decide to define it, is the molecule. It is comprised of elements in combination with other elements to form the single smallest, stable building block of Society. It is also the smallest sphere that we can affect, whether as a preeminent member of that block or as the most modest member. The family is the hidden asset of Society; it introduces ancestral values that lie outside the Social Contract—morals, religion, traditions—which guide each of its members in how they structure everyday life and how they choose to interact with each other as well as other members of Society. It determines what they believe is important to those in their immediate sphere of influence. While it does not—cannot—impact Society in insofar as any one belief does not take any precedence over the beliefs of others, family is a critical and indispensable aspect in maintaining, through Right action, the continuum of our Society. In this respect, the value of one exceeds its seemingly discrete boundaries and spills over into the many. Particularly, people of good Reputation and in whom we place our Trust tend to serve as social beacons around which we congregate. But more than that, they are people around who we can rally. From this, one can effectively resonate beyond self and, being born of Right behavior, echo through the ripples emanating from a single source. We should never underestimate the power of one.

In trying to quickly hobble the Republic together in the wake of the Treaty of Paris (1783) and under less than ideal political and financial circumstances, our founders knew as Hobbes knew that elected officials in a democracy would first look to their private interests before entertaining the interests of others, in this case the State or the Republic, whichever the official represented. Their hope—their "ace-in-the-hole"—was literacy, a by-product of a mostly Protestant populace dating from the mid-1600s. Furthermore, the Constituency of the time was rather well-educated for those days, and our founders relied on that education and the aftermath of eight years of war to keep the attention of the common citizen focused on preserving and advancing the Republic's liberties and minimizing the involvement of Government. Progress, however slow, advanced on the back of this premise and laid the foundations that still support the Republic in which we now inhabit. Throughout our evolution, literacy and a basic education have been the mainstays of the Constituency's power to participate and moderate Government and its policies.

As Society became more enamored with its new found free time, it gladly relegated the course of its liberties to the professional politician. Interrupted by the occasional war or communal disaster (when we, no matter how divided, can seem to put aside all our differences and can rally together like no other country on the face of this planet), Americans have exhibited a tendency to retreat from things political and, instead, prefer to bask in the revelry that those self-same politics were meant to provide.

As we move to take back the reins foolishly ceded to our apathy, it is crucial that we understand how our Social Contract directs our focus and, by extension, our efforts. We need to understand the role we play and the role we allot Government to play. Moreover, we need to walk forward knowing, in the deepest depths of our beings, that Society and our Social Contract drives Government not *vice versa.* To wit, we ought not expect our duly elected representatives in the Government of the Republic to be more beholden to those that elected them rather than to the affairs of the Republic. We expect them to be of good

Reputation, be Responsible, and to be worthy of our Trust in determining the affairs of the Republic wherein, sometimes, those affairs can, regrettably, be contrary to those affairs of an individual State. Likewise, when we look to our duly elected representatives in the Government of the State, we expect them to be of good Reputation, be Responsible, and worthy of our Trust in the affairs that affect the social microcosm of the State. And so on down to the community level. Once we are able to grasp the function of our duly elected representatives, we are better positioned to manage our own expectations of them, better able to petition them, and better qualified to oversee them.

Our ladder society is partially a consequence of America's brand of capitalism making it, for the most part, self-regulating. What the market can bear changes from time to time thus affecting our worth and thereby our position on that ladder. In changing markets, we can move either up or down. Much of what determines this is whether or not we, as individuals, are good custodians of what we possess both materially and essentially. What is certain is that as supply and demand change so does the value—and more specifically the cost—of varying goods and services. When values/costs change, we must, after a Reasonable and candid reflection of our worth and desired quality of life, decide if we opt to receive the benefits of those goods and services. As such, the onus is upon the individual. Just as Society does not share in your personal exploitation of these goods and services neither is it responsible for your burden if those goods and services prove too costly. While we do exercise

Compassion to assist Constituents who, from time to time and under conditions previous elucidated, experience the occasional hardship that may accompany a drastically changing market, we do not condone an atmosphere of something-for-nothing.

Yet we hear recent mutterings of providing certain services "free" which hereinto have been subject to market fluctuations *viz.* supply and demand. We must rout these ideas from our Society insofar as those services do not affect our security, safety, or infrastructure. All else lies outside the purview of our Social Contract and we are loathed to upend our Social Contract in favor of a Socialist one; particularly, as we have historically seen a large number of endeavors in that vein fail in countries with diverse populations mostly due to either economic or social unsustainability or both. We should not forget that the provision of "free" services must come from the resources of Government which resources, in turn, are supplied by Society. And as an interesting sidebar: When something is free its value is zero beyond its obvious utility. It cannot be bought or sold. It can be used, but more likely it would be *abused* since one could use it in any fashion destroying its intrinsic usefulness because another of the same kind could be appropriated at no cost. This is all rendered moot when we remember that our Society has been built upon capitalism. As such, we are compelled to value goods and service accordingly.

This leads us to question how some of us find ourselves in such dire economic quandaries. The simple answer is "decisions." We need to be prudent in the decisions we make, particularly those that have the potential to spill over into the rest of Society. Being better informed about the immediate and long-term consequences of our decisions help ensure that we profit from our choices and minimize the odds of negative repercussions both to ourselves and to Society. For example: It fails the common-sense test to spend $200,000 for a college degree in art history without first understanding what is—if any—the return on that investment and nominally how long it will take to achieve that return. An imprudent decision does not add value to an individual's potential worth nor does long-term financial hardship lend itself to a good quality of life. Whatever short-term rewards one may perceive come at a price that can prove itself unbearable over one's lifetime. It is not in our Social Contract to take on the burden of that individual nor is it in the interest of Society to repeatedly re-enforce such failure. Instead, we—as much as we can—need to make informed, well-thought out, Emotionless decisions and encourage those in our sphere of influence to do the same. When we do thusly, we serve as an example that extends beyond our universe of one and inspires others to do likewise.

To restore our Social Contract is to invoke the power of one; of the individual. It is a simple two-step process: Realization and Actualization. Realization is to acknowledge who we are as a Society and what basic characteristics set us apart from other societies. We are an individualized, socially mobile ladder society, competitive in nature, amassing materials goods as a means of defining status, and exercising pride as a measure of self-worth. If any of us cannot abide with that assessment, if any of us cannot commit to our Social Contract within these confines, or if any one of us feels that their individual morals, values, or beliefs must be adopted by the rest of Society in order for them to be content, then perhaps it would behoove them to emigrate to another society that more adequately conforms to their world view. For the rest of us, we need to be comfortable in our own social skin.

The second step is Actualization; that is, the execution of our obligations under the Social Contract of which the most urgent is to do what is Right. When we dedicate ourselves to Right behavior, we stop seeing our Society in its sundry elements—whites, blacks, Latinos, Catholics, Muslims, Protestants, Buddhist, Hindi, rich, poor, southerners, northerners, city people, country people, tall, short, men, women, heterosexual, homosexual—and see it as a single organism that provides the fabric of all our liberties and underwrites the protections that allow us, as individuals, to pursue lives of opportunity, contentment, and fulfillment. And hopefully along the way, some measure of happiness.

If each of us could wake up tomorrow and dedicate ourselves to this process, a *tsumani* of social reconciliation would follow. But it is up to each of us as individuals to make this solemn commitment, for it is in those dark, private places where, unobserved, doing the Right thing is most difficult. It is easy when we have an audience to applaud us, but when it's just ourselves, Emotion and Want and bias all begin speaking to us until the sound of Reason and Compassion are no longer heard.

But like physical exercise, the more we do Right, the easier it becomes; the stronger we become.

The future of our Society is on your shoulders, dear reader. If you choose to reject our Social Contract and proceed further in anarchy, we will surely implode under our divisiveness like so many failed and extinct dynasties that have gone before us. Should this happen we cannot point our fingers at our neighbors saying, "Well he did it, too." Bad behavior in others is no excuse for bad behavior in ourselves. It would be a travesty to succumb to ruination and loss of liberty only to find out on the other side that it was all avoidable but for our resistance to or rejection of, perhaps, the simplest Social Contract that ever existed.

Do what is Right. Exercise Compassion. Be of good Reputation so that those in your sphere of influence honor you with their Trust. Be Responsible in the exercise of your Power. Do not infringe the liberties of your neighbor. Doubt not that these qualities are beyond you. After all, you are an Ameri*can*, not an Ameri*can't*.

Bibliography

1. Aristotle. *Politics*. 350 BCE

2. Arkowitz, Hal and Lilienfeld, Scott. "Why Science Tells Us Not to Rely on Eyewitness Accounts." *Scientific American*. January 2010.

3. Brackley, Dean. "Downward Mobility: Social Implications of St. Ignatius's Two Standards." *Studies in the Spirituality of Jesuits*. January 1988.

4. Carlyle, Thomas. *The French Revolution: A History*. 1837.

5. Carlyle, Thomas. *On Heroes and Hero Worship*. 1841.

6. Center for Disease Control. Vital Statistics of the United States, 1966. Vol II Sec 5

7. Center for Disease Control. NCHS Data Visualization Gallery (www.cdc.gov/nchs/data-visualization/mortality-trends/index.htm). Mortality Trends in the United States, 1900-2017.

8. Center for Disease Control. "United States Life Tables, 2017 (Table A)." National Vital Statistics Report. Vol 68 No 7.

9. Descartes, Rene. *Discourse on Method and Meditations on First Philosophy*. 1637.

10. Descartes, Rene. *Meditations: First Philosophy*. 1641.

11. De Tocqueville, Alexis. *De La Democratie en Amerique* (Democracy in America). 1835.

12. DiMasi, JA. "Assessing Pharmaceutical Research and Development Costs." *JAMA Intern Med.* 2018; 178(4): 587

13. Donohue, John and Levitt, Steven. "The Impact of Legalized Abortion on Crime." *The Quarterly Journal of Economics*. Vol CXVI Issue 2 May 2001.

14. Ellis, Joseph J. *The Quartet: Orchestrating the Second American Revolution, 1783-1789*. Vintage. 2015.

15. Forssman, Hans and Thuwe, Inga. "One Hundred and Twenty Children Born After Application for Therapeutic Abortion Refused." *Acta Psychiatrica Scandinavica*. (71-78) 1966.

16. *Groundhog Day*. Dir. Harold Ramis. 1993. Film.

17. Garner, Bryan. *Black's Law Dictionary*. Thomson Reuters. Tenth Edition.

18. Halpern and Pastores. "Critical care medicine beds, use, occupancy and costs in the United States: a methodological review." *Critical Care Med.* 2015 Nov: 43(11); 2452-2459.

19. Hobbes, Thomas. *Leviathan or The Matter, Forme, and Power of a Common-Wealth Ecclesiastical and Civil*. 1651.

20. H.R. 1865, Division A, Title V, General Provisions. Public Law 116-94 §506.

21. H.R. 2518 – 103rd Congress (1993-1994)

22. Lewis, C.S. *Mere Christianity*. Harper. 1952.

23. Lott, John Jr and Whitley, John. "Abortion and Crime: Unwanted Children and Out-of-Wedlock Births." *Economic Inquiry*. Vol 45 No 2 (304-324) April 2007.

24. *Order of R.R. Telegraphers v. Railway Express Agency*. 321 US 342, 348-49, 64 S. Ct. 582,586. 1944.

25. Rockefeller Commission Report. *Population and the American Future: The Report of the Commission on Population Growth and the American Future*. (Chap 11) 1968.

26. *Roe v. Wade*, 410 U.S. 113 (1973)

27. Rousseau, Jean-Jacques. *A Discourse on the Moral Effects of Arts and Sciences*. 1750.

28. Rousseau, Jean -Jacques. *The Social Contract.* 1762.

29. Santayana, George. *The Life of Reason*. Volume 1. 1905.

30. *Toussle v. US*, 397 US 112, 90 S. Ct. 858. 1970

31. Unborn Victims Act. United States Code: Title 18, Chapter 1 (Crimes) §1841. Title 10, Chapter 22 (Uniform Code of Military Justice) §919a.

32. Voltaire. *Notebooks*. ca 1735-1750.

33. Zhuang Zhou. *Zhuangzi*. Unknown.

About the Author

Many young boys dream of growing up to be a superhero, and Mark was no exception. He spent much of his youth honing these skills leaping throughout the Canajoharie gorge, cooking up squirrels, and spending many evenings trying to start campfires with sticks and stones. But he always returned home Sunday morning in time to be an altar boy at the local Catholic Church. There were a few BB gunfights down by the Snakehole and many other escapades with Dave, his faithful comrade-in-arms and brother. When he realized high school graduation was not optional, he spent his senior year lunch breaks experimenting in the physics lab making up for the classes he skipped. Mark graduated with honors and continued his education at Clarkson University.

He joined the Army hoping to become Captain America but also to earn enough money to complete his four-year degree in Electrical Engineering. Upon graduation he continued to serve his country as a medic. He departed the Army as a commissioned officer in the Signal Corps. He proceeded across this great Country on his motorcycle and found a resting place in Colorado where he started over in life as a dishwasher working his way up to a *sous* chef at a three-star restaurant while exploring religions outside of Catholicism. He landed a position as a field service engineer, thanks to his EE degree from Clarkson University, and was able to travel much of the United States and Europe repairing machinery and seeing the world. Wanting to further pursue his practice in martial arts, he moved to Fuji, Japan to study Aikido. After arriving in Japan, he found a position as an English teacher. He departed Japan 15 years later, with a black belt in aikido, having played locally in a Japanese folk rock band, and having worked in business development for a well-known Japanese pharmaceutical company in order to take a position in Boston as Vice President of Business Development for the American subsidiary of a Japanese pharmaceutical company.

Mark continues to work in the pharmaceutical business out of his cabin with his much-loved, four-legged companion Maggie. His varied experiences domestically and internationally have deepened his desire for the freedoms that created our United States.

—Barbara Corrigan, CPA, MBA
September 2020

Made in the USA
Columbia, SC
28 April 2022

59650960R00113